The New Lean

In today's rapidly changing business landscape, organizations are challenged not only to adapt to evolving market dynamics but to excel in the face of uncertainty. Continuous improvement emerges as a strategic imperative, offering a systematic approach to enhance processes, boost efficiency, and drive innovation. This book delves into the heart of continuous improvement, providing a roadmap for organizations to navigate their journey toward maturity. The continuous improvement maturity model (CIMM) described in this book is not just a framework, but a holistic guide designed to support organizations in assessing and advancing their continuous improvement capabilities. As the author embarks on this exploration, he presents an approach that spans from foundational practices to advanced strategies. CIMM is a versatile tool adaptable to diverse industries, sectors, and organizational sizes.

The key components of CIMM are:

- **Integration with Best Practices**—CIMM is not designed in isolation. We highlight its compatibility with established continuous improvement methodologies such as Lean, Six Sigma, Change Management, and Leadership Attributes. Learn how to leverage existing best practices while embracing the unique contributions of CIMM.
- **Practical Application**—Real-world examples and practical insights illustrate how organizations have successfully applied CIMM to overcome challenges, drive innovation, and achieve sustainable excellence. These stories offer inspiration and guidance for your own journey.

The New Lean

The Modern Approach to Continuous Improvement

Kyle Toppazzini

Routledge
Taylor & Francis Group
A PRODUCTIVITY PRESS BOOK

First published 2024
by Routledge
605 Third Avenue, New York, NY 10158

and by Routledge
4 Park Square, Milton Park, Abingdon, Oxon, OX14 4RN

Routledge is an imprint of the Taylor & Francis Group, an informa business

ISBN: 978-1-032-78647-6 (hbk)
ISBN: 978-1-498-73598-8 (pbk)
ISBN: 978-1-315-36962-4 (ebk)

DOI: 10.4324/9781315369624

Typeset in Minion
by SPi Technologies India Pvt Ltd (Straive)

This book is dedicated to my beautiful wife and the love of my life,
Jennifer Lahti, who has provided the support, encouragement,
and love required to complete this book.

Contents

Preface xii
Acknowledgments xiv
Author xv

Chapter 1 Why Lean and Transformation Projects Fail to Implement a Culture of Continuous Improvement 1

Cultural Change—Transforming the DNA of the Organization 19
Change Management—Guiding the Transformation Process 21
Leadership Attributes—Guiding the Culture of Continuous Improvement 22
McKinsey Study: Linking Effective Change Implementation, Continuous Improvement, and Strategy Execution 24
The McKinsey Study 24
Implications for Building a Culture of Continuous Improvement 25
Notes 26

Chapter 2 Bridging the Gap Between Lean and Continuous Improvement 28

Bridging the Gap Between Traditional Lean Efforts and Continuous Improvement 33
Understanding the Gap: Traditional Lean and Continuous Improvement 34
Fundamental Principles for Bridging the Gap 36
Key Changes Needed for Bridging the Gap 38
Shifting from Process Optimization to a Culture of Improvement 42
Illustrating a Roadmap to Embrace a Culture of Ongoing Progress 45
Notes 50

Chapter 3 The New Lean—A Fresh New Approach to Lean Deployment and Continuous Improvement 51

Unveiling the Narrative of Success 51
Transforming Organizations and Unlocking Their Potential with Lean Six Sigma and CIMM 53
The Power of Fusing Perceptions with Facts for Business Success 55
The Journey to Lean Thinking and Data-Driven Decision-Making 57

Chapter 4 A New Lean—A Fresh Approach to Continuous Improvement 60

Foundations of CIMM: A Confluence of Disciplines 60
Lean Methodologies: A Framework of Efficiency and Value 60
Change Management Strategies: Navigating the Tides of Transformation 61
Journeying Through the CIMM Stages: From Conception to Excellence 61
Stage 1: Lean Initiation—Laying the Foundation for Transformation 61
Stage 2: Lean Assimilation—Nurturing a Culture of Continuous Improvement 62
Stage 3: Lean Mastery—Navigating Change with Proficiency 64
Stage 4: Lean Transformation—Achieving Sustainable Excellence 65
Impact in Action: Research and Real-World Application 67
Initiating Cultural Shifts: A Catalyst for Transformation 68
Cultural Transformation: The Heart of Progress 68
Practical Steps for Cultural Transformation 68
The Process at Various Stages 68
Effective Change Management: Navigating Transition with Precision 69
Change Management: A Prerequisite for Success......70

Step-by-Step Approach to Change Management....70
The Process at Various Stages....70
Nurturing Leadership for Continuous Improvement: The Catalysts of Progress....71
Leadership: The North Star of Transformation....71
Developing Leadership Qualities: A Guided Journey....71
The Process at Various Stages....72
Empowering Organizations for Sustained Growth and Agility Through CIMM....73
Creating a Culture of Continuous Improvement....73
Integration of Lean and Change Management for Synergistic Impact....73
Adaptability and Agile Responses....75
Empowering Frontline Employees as Influencers....76
Measurement, Learning, and Evolution....78
Embedding CIMM in Organizational DNA....78
Notes....82

Chapter 5 Results from Using the CIMM Framework....83

Harnessing the Power of CIMM: Real-World Examples of Global Organizations....84
General Electric's Resurgence....84
Toyota's Manufacturing Excellence....86
Amazon's Customer-Centric Innovation....87
Transformative Impact of the CIMM Framework on Local Business Ventures....88
Streamlining Operations at Acme Manufacturing....88
Empowering Excellence at Stellar Call Center....89
Statistical Evidence: Concrete Results of CIMM Adoption....92
Anecdotal Narratives: Real-Life Triumphs of CIMM Adoption....93
Quantifiable Success Stories: Measuring CIMM's Impact....97

Chapter 6 Model Scalability and Global Considerations....................102

Scalability of the CIMM....................103
Understanding the CIMM....................103
The Essence of Scalability....................105
Challenges and Considerations....................106
Balancing Flexibility and Standardization....................108
Global Implications of CIMM Scalability....................109
Enabling Sustainable Growth....................111
Adaptability of the CIMM Model to Different Organizational Structures and Cultures....................112
Organizational Structures: One Size Does Not Fit All....................112
Navigating Cultural Diversity....................114
Strategies for Successful Adaptation....................115
Implementing CIMM in Diverse Settings—Tailoring for Success....................117
Recognizing Diverse Business Environments....................117
Tailoring CIMM for Success....................119
Applying CIMM Globally: Cultivating Cross-Cultural Continuous Improvement....................122
Cultural Intelligence—A Foundation for Success....................122
Case Study of McDonald's Corporation: Streamlining Processes Worldwide....................124
Case Study of BASF SE—Leveraging Global Network for Innovation....................125
From Traditional Lean to CIMM: A Paradigm Shift in Continuous Improvement....................127
Traditional Lean Methodologies—The Foundation....................127
Limitations of Traditional Lean—Navigating Constraints....................128
Enter CIMM—A New Approach to Continuous Improvement....................129
Cultural Shift, Change Management, and Adaptive Leadership: Pillars of Sustainable Continuous Improvement....................131
Cultural Shift—Nurturing the Foundation....................131

Change Management—Guiding the Transformation 133
Adaptive Leadership—Guiding Transformational Change 134
Synchronizing the Pillars for Success—A Holistic Approach to Excellence 136

Bibliography 139

Index 141

Preface

Welcome to *The New Lean: Fresh New Approach to Continuous Improvement*. This book is a culmination of extensive research, practical insights, and a collective effort to guide organizations on their path to achieving excellence through continuous improvement.

THE CONTINUOUS IMPROVEMENT IMPERATIVE

In today's rapidly changing business landscape, organizations are challenged to not only adapt to evolving market dynamics but to excel in the face of uncertainty. Continuous improvement emerges as a strategic imperative, offering a systematic approach to enhance processes, boost efficiency, and drive innovation. This book delves into the heart of continuous improvement, providing a roadmap for organizations to navigate their journey toward maturity.

A MODEL FOR EXCELLENCE

Our continuous improvement maturity model (CIMM) is not just a framework but a holistic guide designed to support organizations in assessing and advancing their continuous improvement capabilities. As we embark on this exploration, we present an approach that spans from foundational practices to advanced strategies. CIMM is a versatile tool adaptable to diverse industries, sectors, and organizational sizes.

KEY COMPONENTS

1. **Integration with Best Practices**: CIMM is not designed in isolation. We highlight its compatibility with established continuous improvement

methodologies such as Lean, Six Sigma, Change Management, and Leadership Attributes. Learn how to leverage existing best practices while embracing the unique contributions of CIMM.

2. **Practical Application**: Real-world examples and practical insights illustrate how organizations have successfully applied CIMM to overcome challenges, drive innovation, and achieve sustainable excellence. These stories offer inspiration and guidance for your own journey.

NAVIGATING YOUR CONTINUOUS IMPROVEMENT JOURNEY

Whether you are a seasoned practitioner, a C-suite executive, or a newcomer to the world of continuous improvement, this book provides actionable insights and practical tools to navigate your organization's path toward excellence. Our goal is to empower you to embrace continuous improvement as a culture, a mindset, and a strategic advantage.

CONCLUSION

As you turn the pages of *The New Lean*, envision the possibilities that continuous improvement holds for your organization. May this journey through the CIMM inspire and guide you to reach new heights of operational excellence.

Welcome to a transformative exploration of continuous improvement.

Kyle Toppazzini
December 2023

Acknowledgments

I want to say a special thank you to the publisher at Taylor and Francis Publishing, who has provided me with all the support, patience, and guidance that I needed to make this book a success. I also want to thank Lisa Mininni, the president of Excellerate Associates, who has provided me with support and guidance in writing this book and making it a success. I want to also thank my brother Keith Toppazzini for all his support throughout this process. I also want to thank my wife Jennifer lahti for all her love encouragement and support in taking this journey.

Author

Mr Kyle Toppazzini has conducted 100 process improvement and Lean Six Sigma projects. Many of these projects utilize Lean Six Sigma methodologies and philosophies. Mr Toppazzini's track record includes an identified 26 million dollars in cost savings, an 80% improvement in productivity and quality, and a reduction in process time by 80%.

In addition, Mr Toppazzini has been training in Lean, Six Sigma, and Lean Six Sigma methods since 2000. He has developed yellow, green, and black belt training (online and classroom) and trained more than 1000 people from multiple organizations (including Charles Schwab) and countries at all levels on Lean Six Sigma concepts.

1

Why Lean and Transformation Projects Fail to Implement a Culture of Continuous Improvement

Make your workplace into a showcase that can be understood by everyone at a glance.

—Taiichi Ohno[1]

What is the first word crossing your mind when I say Lean transformation? Well, you might think about customer value and organizing waste material. And you are right up to an extent, but Lean transformation is much more critical and has bigger consequences on the organization, eventually translating to society. Lean transformation has a continuous effect rather than discrete; it might sound more like a nuance, but making the distinction is imperative.

If we look at Lean transformation only from the perspective of the waste-reducing framework or cost-cutting model, then, actually, we are perplexed and underestimating the essence of this innovative phenomenon. By incorporating the essential elements of Lean transformation, any organization can smoothly implement a culture of continuous improvement. Unfortunately, hundreds of organizations have failed to do so.

Implementing significant changes within organizations has historically proven to be challenging, with abundant research indicating that most transformation efforts do not succeed. In the present fast-paced context, the difficulty is compounded by the need for swift adaptations to market fluctuations, external disruptions, and the demands of novel business frameworks. The risks associated with these changes have become more elevated than in the past.

DOI: 10.4324/9781315369624-1

In both academic studies and real-world applications, it has been observed that transformations are most likely to succeed when they concentrate on four main actions to alter attitudes and actions. These actions include promoting comprehension and belief, strengthening changes through official methods, enhancing skills and abilities, and providing role models. These concepts, collectively known as the "influence model," were first presented over a decade ago in a *McKinsey Quarterly* piece titled "The Psychology of Change Management." They were formulated based on scholarly research and hands-on knowledge of what proved effective and what didn't.

But why has it happened frequently, and why have companies miserably failed to achieve sustainable continuous improvement? Let's figure this out by learning all we can about this results-driven approach.

To start with, let's wrap our heads around the meaning of Lean transformation. In simple words, it is a systematic approach that is precisely used to solve organizational challenges by implementing small changes. The fundamental motive of Lean transformation is decluttering. Now, you must be wondering if we are talking about an enormous organization or a personal closet. Well, just like decluttering shapes your personal closet, it does wonders for organizational operations. Lean transformation amplifies the delivery of value by moving away from conventional business methods. Ultimately, redundant activities are identified and later eliminated. In this way, all the attention and resources are directed toward the important activities and consequently lift the company.

> The critical first question for any Lean transformation is: which activities create value and which are a form of waste? Once.
>
> **—Eric Ries**[2]

So, here is a question: Can companies survive without Lean transformation? Surprisingly, the answer is yes. But can the company boom without it? Definitely not. In other words, it's not only about the survival mechanism but also about flourishing and prospering as a community. In the long run, implementing Lean transformation can elevate society. It helps companies to acclimatize to the latest trends, staying agile and resilient against all odds. It enables all sorts of organizations to create a sustainable, value-oriented culture while meeting the customer's requirements. All these strategies have a focal point to promote sustainable and continuous development.

Before diving into a more deep and thoughtful study of Lean transformation, let's discuss its history and how the model evolved. Lean transformation was developed in Japan, a society with a very different work ethic than the West.

> Japanese attitudes toward work seem to be critically different from American attitudes.
>
> **—Akio Morita**[3]

Lean transformation framework, which has its origins in the Toyota Production System (TPS), seeks to achieve these goals by emphasizing the elimination of extra steps and the maximization of existing resources. Respect for authority, discipline among peers, and a commitment to harmony are hallmarks of Japanese culture. The Japanese work ethic has always emphasized loyalty and respect for one's superiors. Cultural norms of natural deference like these inspire perseverance and cooperation. Lean concepts, which emphasize reducing waste and working together for the greater objective, are an incredible fit for this cultural milieu.

Individualism and a more combative attitude toward authority are more common in the West. A higher level of resistance to change among workers may result from this. Changes in attitude and methods that are necessary for a successful Lean transformation are sometimes met with cynicism and resistance in Western businesses. However, with certain tweaks, the Lean transformation methodology has been effectively implemented in Western contexts.

Companies have learned to strike a balance between fostering respect for authority and encouraging employee involvement, acknowledging the cultural variances that exist. Successful transitions have been facilitated by strategies like open channels of communication, employee participation in decision-making, and highlighting the advantages of Lean approaches.

In a nutshell, Japan's cultural nuances of esteem and respect for authority play a significant role in explaining the genesis of Lean transformation there. The employee–employer relationship may be viewed differently in Eastern cultures, but the fundamentals of Lean can still be applied successfully with some creative modification. To ensure the success of Lean transformations across a wide range of organizational contexts, it is essential to recognize these cultural differences and adapt implementation tactics accordingly.

I assume that we all now comprehend Lean transformation and its significance in the corporate sector. But how do we enforce it? Whether you are planning to impose it on a small team, a particular department, or a full-fledged organization, the Lean transformation model has five key focus areas to navigate.

1. Situational approach: First and foremost, you must analyze the situation and ask yourself a few questions: Why am I applying this? What's the purpose? What are the expected results? And what if I failed to acquire the estimated outcomes? What are the alternatives? Before incorporating Lean transformation, you should get the officials and senior management on board. Before reverting to the former policies, you should be transparent in pinpointing the challenges and problems that you want to get rid of by incorporating the Lean transformation model.
2. Capability advancement: By answering the question "How are we building capability?", you can gain insight into your team's strengths and weaknesses and prioritize skillset development. It's crucial to ensure that both managers and regular team members receive training in Lean practices. Without a shift in mindset and work approach, any desired changes won't be possible.
3. Accountable leadership: Lean transformation focuses on building responsible leaders. Effective leaders encourage their team members to become more self-sufficient and organized while also promoting ongoing growth and development. By fostering a culture of shared leadership, individuals are able to recognize their own potential and take on more responsibilities. Providing team members with the freedom to make decisions without constantly seeking approval from a supervisor is essential to ensure that Lean transformation is successful.
4. Practical mindset: In order to effectively implement Lean methodology within your organization, it is crucial to evaluate your current organizational culture and mindset. This will help you identify any missing values or necessary changes that need to be made. Transforming your company's culture to align with Lean principles is a necessary step for a successful Lean implementation.
5. Improvement in process: Evaluating the processes that require optimization and presenting a list of improvements is one of the principles of the Lean transformation model. Clearly communicating

the expected changes during and after Lean transformation is vital to avoid resistance. Answering the question "How are we improving the current work?" can assist in this communication.

So, how do you put into action a Lean transformation in your organization? The first stage in restructuring your organization is to familiarize yourself with the Lean transformation paradigm. Due to the prolonged nature of the procedure, you should plot out your next steps in advance. A typical Lean transformation plan consists of eight steps:

1. Evaluation: Conduct an analysis to determine the root causes of the issues and the best ways to address them. At this stage, you face a crucial decision of whether to roll out Lean gradually or dive headfirst into sweeping, systemic changes.
2. Initiation: Launch an initiative to win over the upper management and acquire the resources for the transformation.
3. Training and gearing: Invest in management staff training and new tools. Finding a consultant who can give you hands-on experience with the tools you need and guide you through the Lean implementation process may be necessary.
4. Flow inside a single service: In the context of a company, a service is a function that takes in some input, processes it, and then returns some output. Getting the most out of Lean transformation requires a clear visual of the input, process, and output loop. At this point in your plan, you should explain the idea of value stream mapping, a method for visually depicting your team's processes in preparation for continuous improvement.
5. Analyze and optimize: Look closely at your current workflow to determine where else you could be making progress. Establishing uniform key performance indicators (KPIs) for your process and getting the whole company on board with them is an important step in Lean transformation.
6. Flow through various connected services: Value stream mapping should be implemented throughout the entire organization, beginning with product management and ending with the direct transfer of value to the consumer.
7. Establishing regulating mechanisms: When you have a full value stream in place, you'll need a standardized approach to managing it. At this point, having a method like Portfolio Kanban that makes

all company processes visible across all levels of management can be invaluable.

8. Enhancing operations and delivery consistently: Finally, make a culture of constant development a part of your business's DNA. Everyone should take it to heart and always be on the lookout for opportunities to hone their skills and advance the process.

By applying these eight steps, you can ace the implementation of Lean transformation into the organization and will accumulate ample benefit from it. For the application of the model, you must understand the key points of a Lean transformation. Let me demonstrate the factors that should be considered while planning to incorporate the model. Primarily, you must win over your audience. But what does that mean? Winning from whom? It means that you must remember that rather than just a framework, model, or roadmap, Lean is a way of life; it's a culture to fetch personal and professional success. Therefore, it is your responsibility to persuade your staff that the Lean transformation model is beneficial and extensively practical. In other words, it is a shift in perspective.

But, how do you convince team members about the advantages of the Lean transformation model? Lean leaders should educate the members that their participation and backing are necessary for the success of several Lean manufacturing tools individually. You can't pick and choose when you want your staff to halt production in the event of an issue; it must be done consistently—maintaining a steady rate of output calls for regular monitoring of those responsible for it. Global ideas like Plan Do Check Act (PDCA) and continuous improvement fail instantly without widespread support from the workforce.

Therefore, once more, you must win over your people! You can't win over everyone either. No way this can happen. If you take a straw poll of ten workers, you're likely to find at least one who is opposed to the novel concept and perhaps the business as a whole. But, you'd need the backing of the vast majority of your country's citizens.

But is there a secret to persuading your team members? The question now is how to win over it. Pressure, threats of unemployment, and excessive workload are not effective methods of persuasion, as is evident in the past. This seems like it would be common sense to all managers, but clearly not. One common method is to just come out and say it: This is crucial. Do something like putting up posters. You could, for instance, organize a meeting to get the squad on board with the new policies.

This strategy, too, is rarely successful. A lot of people in business have learned to tune out the CEOs' speeches and focus instead on what their actions reveal about the company's leadership. Managers sometimes exaggerate the impact of their utterances. Therefore, such verbal practice is typically ineffective. Based on the outcome of the few programs in the past advertised using similar language, such talks or posters may play only a supporting function, at best, or turn the people against it, at worst. A banner advertising the fourth great program is likely to be met with hostility if the previous plans and strategies have only served to increase the chaos.

The greater the level of trust between management and staff, the less difficult it will be. A Lean transformation will be more challenging for a corporation that practices management by fear. However, a Lean transformation model can be accomplished even if management is only moderately admired by staff. If done well, it has the potential to boost management's standing as well.

The implementation of Lean transformation demands baby steps rather than abrupt change. At first, Lean leaders don't need their conviction; just their willingness to give it a shot will do. So, to test the waters, see if you can get them on board with an enhancement project. Choose a situation that will interest the staff and has a good possibility of being resolved. You can use this accomplishment as a stepping stone for future initiatives. The greater your success rate with such a tactic, the more people will put their faith in it.

The next step is to get your team engaged. Employee participation in Lean transformation is also essential because it will have a significant impact on their work. The implementation of this strategy has two key benefits that should not be overlooked. First, your likelihood of succeeding is improved. Use their insight to confirm the effectiveness of the modification. Involve them in all crucial decisions and make them feel special and important. It is tried and tested that such employees give their 100% efforts and offer more than the manager of officials demands. Second, if employees are included in Lean transformation, they will be more likely to trust the new system. People have a natural skepticism of top-down, imposed solutions, and they're usually right to be wary of such approaches.

Obviously, it would be impossible to get everyone on board with Lean transformation at once because this only applies to specific manufacturing companies. A group size of 5—12 individuals works well, depending on the nature of the discussion. For example, the members of management, engineering, maintenance, and, most importantly, operators should all be present. In terms of operators, there tends to be a small number of influential leaders in each department. Including them in problem-solving efforts and giving them a voice would do wonders for the morale of the entire facility.

At the end of the day, the initiatives also need to be good for the people working on them. For example, General Motors (GM) believed it would be in the company's best interest to lay off 25% of the workforce, but the employees disagreed. In the beginning, it's especially important to prioritize projects that would improve production. Finally, you need buy-in from the upper management. Managers typically entrust work to subordinates. After all, leading people is one of their main responsibilities.

The company culture, however, cannot be changed by the committee. A Lean transformation requires management support in the form of not just passive permission but also active motivation.

Companies like Trumpf and Porsche, which underwent successful Lean conversions, had top-level managers who not only had the freedom to change but also actively pushed their organization in the right direction—Mathias Kammüller at Trumpf and Taiichi Ohno at Toyota. The former spent considerable time in a Bosch–Japan joint venture, where they were exposed to the Lean methodology. He reformed Trumpf based on what he learned from implementing Lean. This means that upper management needs Lean training as well. This requires not just an intellectual understanding of kanban but also the ability to take the helm on Lean initiatives. The best way to learn Lean is to dive right in. It's similar to learning to ride a bike; the only way to get good at it is to actually ride a bike. Books are of limited use in this situation. A manager's ability to support and drive a Lean transformation increases in proportion to the extent to which he or she embraces and demonstrates the Lean culture.

On the other hand, Lean transformation is more likely to be hampered by management through cost accounting. The value added by Lean projects is not always easy to quantify. In cost accounting, if a number can't be calculated, it's typically not entered. If you accept this "zero," Lean offers no advantage despite the fact that this is not the case. There are numerous things that must be in place before a Lean transformation can begin. The Lean transformation model is a way of life that calls for a radical shift in perspective. Managers shouldn't treat employees like machines; yet, they sometimes do. As with humans, every department has its own unique culture. Not all departments of the company will respond the same way to the same treatment. Improving the culture is not a one-time event but rather an ongoing process that requires effort.

> *"Practice the philosophy of continuous improvement. Get a little bit better every single day."*
>
> **—Brian Tracy**
> *an American motivational speaker and author*[4]

Understanding the Lean transformation model is one thing, but implementing the model is not that easy. When companies start new projects or face any challenges, they are extremely fragile and vulnerable. The company can fall any minute; that is why the correct dimension is as important as the implication. Confused? Let me narrate to you two distinctive stories: one on the successful implication and the other on the failed implication of the Lean transformation model.

There is a plethora of failures while implementing Lean transformation. Plenty of them are unknown due to confidentiality reasons, and if public, only available in the abstract. But the case of GM is widely known. There is adequate information, theories, and analysis that is readily available on the internet about the failure of GM cases. Through their New United Motor Manufacturing Inc. (NUMMI) joint venture with Toyota, they successfully trained a large number of individuals in Lean principles at the source. However, they ultimately failed to capitalize on this success. Despite having numerous mid-level employees highly skilled in Lean methods and hundreds of workers who believed in and trusted Lean, they could not transfer this knowledge to their other plants. This failure is a clear example of what not to do when implementing Lean transformations. While many other companies have struggled with Lean transformations, none have failed despite starting from such a strong position. Let's take a more in-depth look at the entire scenario, shall we?

It all started in the early 1980s when Toyota wanted to start its major overseas project. Toyota selected the United States for its huge plant. To alleviate the risk of failure, the company decided to make it a joint venture. Toyota first approached Ford because, apparently, the CEO of Toyota was inspired by Ford's strategy, but Ford declined the offer. Later, Toyota offered this collaboration to GM, and consequentially, the NUMMI emerged in Fremont, California. The NUMMI turned out to be the worst project of the GM, in fact, the foulest in the history of the United States. Just after two years, in 1982, GM and Toyota had to shut down the project, but later, in 1984, they reopened it, but still it didn't turn out the way it was anticipated.

From the upper perspective, the NUMMI was seen as a golden opportunity for both companies, but they both failed in the worst possible way. Earlier, the difference in work culture was blamed for the failure of the project. Long working hours, communication gaps, and poor planning were also thoroughly discussed. Christoph Roser's book *"Faster, Better, Cheaper" in the History of Manufacturing* linked the failure of the NUMMI with Lean transformation. The book mainly discussed smart manufacturing tools and methods to raise efficiency by minimum resources, time, and materials. In that context, the author discussed that the collapse of the NUMMI was caused by neglecting the Lean transformation framework.

The downfall of the NUMMI started at its beginning. Two plants were decided for the manufacturing purpose, i.e., Van Nuys near Los Angeles and Norwood in Cincinnati. Surprisingly, GM had a unique way of motivating the employees: threatening. They used the phrase *"Let's have them fight each other to the death!"* Yes! You heard it right. They set up a strange competition between the two plants. The plant that would efficiently manufacture will get raised, and the runner-up will be shut down. In short, they used terminating threats. The senior VP of Toyota in North America, Mr. Dennis Cuneo, was Toyota's attorney at that time. He explained the situation by quoting:

> *"The perception that everybody had at that time was that the Toyota Production System just worked people to death. It was just basically, "Speed up!" In fact, I remember the first meeting we had in the union hall with union leadership, and there was this gentleman by the name of Gus Billy. He was sitting at the end of the table, and we were talking about the Toyota Production System and Kaizen, etc. It sounds like a production speed-up to me. It's the whole concept of making all these suggestions, trying to suggest your way out of a job."*

Clearly, the threats create an extremely cynical situation for all the employees. Created havoc and isolation for many employees. Another loophole in the project was the lack of top management interest. Toyota's management and officials were keenly indulged in all the operational activities, whereas GM lacked leadership skills. Cuneo summed up the scenario by stating:

> *"I think it surprised GM. Some of the labor relations staff advised us not to. We took a calculated risk. We knew that the former GM workforce*

needed leadership—and the Shop Committee comprised the natural leaders of that workforce. We had to change their attitudes and opinions. So, we sent the shop committee to Japan for three weeks. They saw firsthand what the TPS was all about. And they came back converted and convinced a skeptical rank and file that this GM Production System wasn't so bad if employees align with top management."

Evidently, GM's managers were capable of successfully executing the NUMMI project, but they messed up in leadership skills. The managers at GM were constantly searching for a quick solution that they could pass on to others to implement. They passed on the concept of Lean to others, who then passed it on again. Some employees had learned about Lean principles through the NUMMI, but they were unable to implement them due to resistance from both management and coworkers. These individuals were also divided into small teams or individuals, which made it difficult to act effectively even if there wasn't as much disinterest and opposition. The disinterested behaviors of GM officials became detrimental to the NUMMI; eventually, they had to call off the project.

There was a vivid difference in the working mechanism of Toyota and GM. Both companies couldn't orient themselves to make the NUMMI successful. When the project was revived in 1984, Toyota took over GM in terms of quality, quantity, and turnover. This case is frequently cited as a prime example of how Toyota can be effectively implemented in a unionized American factory, where employees were accustomed to the established GM culture and the typical contentious interactions between management and labor. According to Cuneo, the crucial factor in achieving success was establishing a sense of trust with the workers.

> We built trust early on with our team members. GM had problems selling the Nova from 1987 to '88, and they substantially cut the orders to our plant. We had to reduce production and were running at about 75% capacity, but we didn't lay anybody off. We put people on kaizen teams and found other useful tasks for them. Of all the things we did at NUMMI, that did the most to establish trust.

So, overall, the project was a mess. GM couldn't implement a Lean transformation model to the NUMMI. The cross-culture working attribute happened to be a huge hurdle to surpass. The competition culture, threatening behavior, and disinterested attitude of officials amplified the chaos.

Consequently, the NUMMI was a monumental failure not only for GM and Toyota but also for US history.

Here, some people get confused and perhaps wonder why Toyota would share its highly secretive Lean manufacturing system with a company like GM. Many diverse factors contributed to the establishment of the partnership. But one factor was that Toyota knew GM was the largest automaker in the world and was having trouble with its production. Raising GM's production standards benefited the neighborhood and the country as a whole, and it also provided Americans with well-paying manufacturing jobs. Executives at Toyota have discussed the idea of repaying the United States for aiding Japan's industrial revival after World War II. This is neither empty rhetoric nor idealistic wishful thinking. That's how much they believe it.

Cuneo claims that the outsourcing of small-car production was the original impetus for GM's participation in the business. More and more information regarding Toyota piqued GM's interest in the NUMMI as a potential testing ground. The TPS has been implemented by hundreds of GM executives, managers, and engineers who have been through the NUMMI. Mike Brewer, an early "Alum" of the NUMMI dispatched by GM to learn the TPS, wrote the Bible for manufacturing based on his experiences touring GM plants in the United States and China. GM has adopted the TPS's "Global Manufacturing System" word for word.

> It took GM over 15 years to fully implement Toyota's recommendations. It took GM around five years of significant effort before the company as a whole began to realize increased productivity and quality. *"The Toyota style is not to create results by working hard. It is a system that says there is no limit to people's creativity. People don't go to Toyota to 'work'; they go there to think."*
>
> **—Taiichi Ohno[5]**

So, now you understand how not to learn and apply Lean transformation of the project. Let's delve into another narrative of a highly successful project that occurred due to the correct implementation of the Lean transformation method, and the rest is history.

We all know that the Japanese automaker Toyota is well known for its cutting-edge production methods, especially its pioneering use of the Lean manufacturing philosophy. This case study analyzes Toyota's successful implementation of Lean transformation, which resulted in increased productivity, decreased waste, and increased value for the company's customers.

The origin of the TPS dates back to the 20th century, when Kiichiro Toyoda, the founder of Toyota, visited Ford's River Rouge Plant in the United States. Although impressed with Ford's assembly-line methods, Toyoda recognized the potential for improvement. In those days, car manufacturers like GM and Ford produced a single car model on an assembly line, resulting in inefficiencies, such as excess inventory and high production costs. To solve these problems, Taiichi Ohno, a Japanese engineer, developed the TPS, which is now considered the industry standard for manufacturing.

The corporation addressed these problems by implementing the TPS-inspired Lean manufacturing practices. The TPS was developed to reduce inefficiencies, maximize the use of available resources, and encourage staff participation in making incremental improvements. The fundamentals of Lean implementation on Toyota were:

1. Just-in-time (JIT) production: Toyota's implementation of JIT production entailed building cars only when customers placed orders. This resulted in less stock on hand, lower storage fees, and increased profits.
2. Motivation: Toyota's employees were motivated to find and fix inefficiencies in their daily work by the company's commitment to the Kaizen philosophy of continuous improvement. All employees felt they had a voice in the company's success, thanks to the emphasis placed on continuous improvement.
3. Regard for individuals: The importance of its employees was central to Toyota's Lean concept. The strategy entailed encouraging workers, getting them involved in addressing problems, and giving them control over their work.
4. Jidoka: It is often known as "Automation with a Human Touch," a theory that enables robots to detect errors and halt production without human intervention. That way, Toyota was able to identify the flaws early, and the manufacturing process could improve overall quality.
5. Poka-Yoke: It is a set of error-proofing systems that Toyota put in place to cut down on manufacturing flaws. Because of this, fewer mistakes were made, leading to higher-quality finished goods.

These were a few of many fundamentals or motives of Toyota to apply Lean transformation for the challenges it was facing. Here are six basic steps that the company applied to incorporate Lean transformation:

1. One of Toyota's first steps was to map the entire production process in order to spot sources of waste, including overproduction, extra trips, and waiting time.
2. Second, Toyota adopted JIT manufacturing. Toyota reorganized its assembly lines to cater to genuine consumer demand. Because of this, production times shrank, storage needs were cut down to a minimum, and output went up.
3. The third step was empowering its employees through Kaizen. Kaizen refers to the continuous improvement of all business activities involving all employees, from the CEO to the assembly-line workers. Toyota encouraged its workers to find and fix ineffective processes. The goal of forming these interdisciplinary groups was to solve pressing issues with creative approaches.
4. Fourth, Toyota implemented Jidoka, or quality control, into its assembly lines. Worker flaw detection and correction training was part of this initiative.
5. Implementing the Poka-Yoke system was the fifth step in Toyota's plan to eliminate human error and faulty products from the manufacturing process. As a result, there was less need for rework, which increased productivity.
6. Step six was a continuous improvement and learning culture. Toyota encouraged employees at all levels to offer suggestions for improving the company. Optimization is continuing, thanks to the established feedback loops.

Were these techniques and strategies effective? Yes, the results of Toyota's Lean transformation were impressive. Toyota was able to drastically cut back on wasteful practices such as stockpiling, shipping, manufacturing flaws, and production overruns.

By applying a Lean transformation approach, better cycle times, shorter lead times, and higher resource utilization are all direct results of implementing Lean practices throughout the production process. Toyota was able to reduce defects and enhance quality due to the newly implemented quality control mechanisms and error-proofing tools. Hence, the profitability and cost reductions improved as a result of less waste and improved efficiency. Greater job happiness and engagement were also the results of Kaizen's emphasis on employee empowerment and the value placed on employees' suggestions. However, Toyota's ability to adapt to fluctuating market conditions and customer tastes improved once it adopted JIT production.

To sum up, the success of Toyota's Lean transformation proves that Lean concepts can be used to dramatically improve production. Toyota's use of JIT production, promotion of a culture of continuous improvement, and encouragement of employee participation in problem-solving led to impressive gains in efficiency, productivity, and quality. Toyota's Lean journey case study demonstrates how Lean concepts can be used to improve operations and increase value for consumers.

> Lean transformation is about giving everybody in the organization the opportunity to do their best every day and to feel completely engaged and fulfilled by the work that they do.
>
> **—Philip Holt**[6]

By comparing the two case studies, I believe the picture is clear now. These two cases provide insight into the challenges faced by companies when trying to adopt new strategies. At this stage, we are able to pinpoint the outcomes of the Lean transformation strategy on companies. To summarize the whole scenario, here are five points that provide the eagle view of why companies failed despite having considerable resources, manpower, and budget.

1. Incompetent strategies: Before starting any project, companies need to establish a clear vision and direction. To achieve this, a well-defined strategy should be put in place that outlines responsibilities, resource allocation, metrics, and timelines. Management needs to prioritize the core elements of the project and decide on the most effective deployment order. Additionally, it is important to determine the starting point and how Lean techniques will be implemented throughout the entire operation. Finally, organizations should anticipate potential problems and plan for recovery scenarios. It is crucial to strike a balance between taking on too much and not doing enough, as either approach can lead to failure.
2. Lack of leadership: Lean transformation demands top-to-bottom involvement for successful execution. Leaders should be firm, aspiring,

resilient, forgiving, empathetic, and flexible and should direct employees to a solution and not be task-oriented. These are the necessary qualities for successful leaders in the organization. For successful companies, at least one Lean leader should be there.

3. Insufficient knowledge: Lean transformation implementation is no joke. However, if the leaders and management work properly, it will definitely show results. They should be knowledgeable enough to understand the technicalities of the process. For Lean transformation to be successful and widespread, there needs to be a substantial amount of knowledge among all individuals. Additionally, both line personnel and staff must possess the necessary expertise. The daily support should come from influential and respected line managers who hold the most responsibility and have the power to carry out changes. Depending solely on an outnumbered staff expert who lacks authority to implement Lean is not a practical approach. Without a robust implementation team, the deployment and implementation may fail before even starting.
4. Neglecting the employees: Employees are the most important part of any organization. Typically, they have more vast working knowledge than their bosses, so it is imperative to take their opinion for the successful execution of the project. When they know their reputation, they feel valued and confident in their work. Ultimately, this practice leads to better productivity. It will improve their performance, well-being, and employee retention.
5. Conflicting metrics: To implement Lean transformation effectively, it is important to have metrics that prioritize the processes involved in creating value and their associated costs. Traditional cost accounting methods like absorption and evaluating individual machine and employee performance can lead to behaviors that are not aligned with Lean principles. Lean accounting, on the other hand, directly connects to financial measures but focuses on the performance of the entire value delivery system. While implementing Lean can be challenging, successful results have been shown when it is done correctly. By avoiding or overcoming potential failure modes, Lean and its elements can be effective. For Lean to be successful in your organization, it is important for executive management to become familiar with Lean principles and serve as successful sponsors. This means applying Lean to your own management processes first in order to understand how to apply it to others.

According to a study conducted in 2007, only 24% of Lean initiatives by companies had yielded significant results. Despite this, a census from the same year revealed that almost 70% of manufacturing plants in the United States were using "Lean manufacturing" as their improvement methodology. However, only 2% of respondents had fully achieved their objectives. In reality, the odds are against manufacturing organizations that pursue this ambitious goal. It requires the convergence of multiple factors to achieve success, with most of them being related to personnel issues rather than the process. The application of tools is generally not the problem, but the behavior of senior leaders determines the success of the initiative.

It is evident that Lean transformation can do wonders within the organization. Lean transformation is a popular approach in today's business world that can have a positive impact on companies. By promoting waste reduction and improving practices, it creates a foundation for successful transformation and stable growth. This approach is closely related to operations management, as it requires the fundamental reorganization of firms and all processes necessary for their development. By implementing a Lean transformation approach, companies can effectively function and continue to grow.

In the world of organizational transformation, my journey has been marked by a relentless pursuit of excellence and a burning desire to reshape the Lean framework. I am the architect of the continuous improvement maturity model, affectionately known as CIMM. This model emerged from a deep understanding of the challenges faced by my clients and the numerous projects I've undertaken. Implementing Lean principles across an entire organization is no small feat; it demands substantial resource allocation. But the real challenge lies in the transition to the elusive stage of Lean, where true continuous improvement thrives.

My model is more organic in its deployments. The rate at which the model is deployed and the organizational culture moves toward continuous improvement more gradual. Typical Lean interventions rely on Kaizen Blitz, which requires 5–10 people to be pulled from their regular jobs for 3–5 days at a time, and the organization struggles with that type of commitment.

My mission was clear: to not only introduce Lean tools but also infuse a culture of continuous improvement into the very DNA of organizations. My journey typically began with a survey, a critical first step in identifying the ideal starting point within an organization. I sought out pockets where motivation ran high, where opportunities for improvement were plentiful, and where individuals were inherently driven to excel. These were the fertile grounds for my transformative work.

The survey I employed was not your run-of-the-mill questionnaire. It delved deep into the emotional side of decision-making. It explored how organizations perceived data: Was it a source of nervousness, an uncharted territory, or simply a gut feeling guide? For those who leaned on instinct rather than information, I took it upon myself to initiate them into the world of data-driven decisions.

I encouraged them to reflect on their perceptions of how their processes operated and the outcomes they produced. Often, these judgments were rooted in personal experiences or limited viewpoints rather than the comprehensive data available. As their guide, I initiated them into the realm of data-driven decision-making, laying the foundation for a monumental shift in mindset.

But my mission was far from complete. I understood that many organizations operated within a matrix view, with functional silos managing processes from their narrow perspective. This fragmented approach often resulted in errors cascading from one department to another, wreaking havoc on the value stream. To remedy this, I introduced the concept of value stream mapping.

Collaborating closely with teams, we meticulously mapped out the entire end-to-end process. I challenged them to identify outcomes and waste within their processes, scrutinizing areas of rework, over-processing, delays, and blockages. Their experiences and perceptions formed a crucial part of this process, but it was the overlay with hard data that truly illuminated the path forward.

Revelations were profound. What was once brushed off as inevitable errors now emerged as glaring bottlenecks. Delivery deadlines were being missed, and the fate of products and services hung in the balance. A paradigm shift was unfolding as my clients began to view the organization from a holistic process perspective, recognizing that the true value lay in the entire end-to-end journey.

With the map in hand and insights at the ready, we embarked on a comprehensive analysis. Teams grappled with the root causes of bottlenecks and defects, comparing their initial perceptions with the stark reality illuminated by the data. These discussions were intense but purposeful, driven by a newfound commitment to deliver real value to customers.

My CIMM had not merely revamped Lean but it had also revolutionized the way organizations operated. It was no longer about isolated tools and techniques; it was about instilling Lean principles deep within the culture. Continuous improvement ceased to be a distant dream; it became an integral part of the organizational fabric.

In my model, I used the survey results and slowly changed how they work and brought them through continuous improvement. Once the first group has entirely made that shift to a continuous improvement culture, they go out and promote this new way of working to their peers in other areas, creating momentum for others to go through the same process.

My journey stands as a testament to the power of understanding, data-driven decision-making, and holistic process thinking. My efforts heralded a Lean revolution where organizations thrived on continuous improvement. I had not just transformed organizations; I had transformed lives, one culture at a time. My legacy was one of reshaping the Lean transformation framework, ensuring that Lean principles didn't just survive but thrived in the ever-evolving landscape of modern business.

One of the key reasons why Lean and transformation projects may falter in their pursuit of a culture of continuous improvement is a failure to adapt to the evolving needs of organizations. In this section, we will delve deeply into how a reimagined Lean framework, incorporating cultural change, change management, and leadership attributes, can drive sustainable continuous improvement.

CULTURAL CHANGE—TRANSFORMING THE DNA OF THE ORGANIZATION

Cultural change is the foundational pillar upon which a culture of continuous improvement rests. Traditional Lean methodologies primarily focus on improving processes and eliminating waste. However, to achieve lasting results, organizations must go beyond optimizing workflows; they must transform their organizational DNA.

The first step in cultural change is recognizing and understanding the existing organizational culture. This involves assessing the values, beliefs, and behaviors that currently prevail within the organization. It's crucial to identify any barriers or resistance to change that may exist.

A culture of continuous improvement thrives on open communication and collaboration. Organizations must create an environment where employees feel comfortable sharing their insights, ideas, and concerns without fear of retribution. This often requires breaking down silos and promoting cross-functional collaboration.

To drive cultural change, employees must be empowered to take ownership of the improvement process. This means providing them with the tools, resources, and autonomy to identify and implement improvements in their own areas of expertise. Empowerment fosters a sense of responsibility and accountability.

Leadership plays a critical role in shaping the culture. Leaders must lead by example, demonstrating their commitment to continuous improvement. They should encourage and support employees in their improvement efforts and provide the necessary guidance and resources.

Cultural change is an ongoing process and thus, organizations should invest in continuous learning and adaptation. This includes providing training and development opportunities for employees to enhance their skills and knowledge. It also means being flexible and adaptable in response to changing circumstances.

To ensure that cultural change is taking hold, organizations need to establish metrics and feedback mechanisms that gauge the effectiveness of cultural change initiatives, such as the number of improvement ideas generated, the moderate rate of implementation, and the impact on KPIs.

Furthermore, to illustrate the practical implementation of cultural change, consider sharing case studies and success stories from organizations that have successfully transformed their cultures. These real-world examples can provide valuable insights and inspiration.

Keep in mind that resistance to cultural change is common. Organizations should anticipate and address resistance by involving employees in the change process, providing clear communication, and addressing concerns and misconceptions.

Organizations should continuously reinforce the desired culture through leadership messaging, recognition and rewards for improvement efforts, and regular cultural assessments. After all, cultural change should not be a short-term initiative but a long-term commitment.

Incorporating cultural change into the Lean framework is essential for ensuring that continuous improvement becomes an integral part of the organization's identity. It shifts the focus from isolated process improvements to a holistic transformation of how the organization operates and innovates. When cultural change is successfully implemented, employees become the driving force behind continuous improvement, ensuring its sustainability and long-term success.

By fostering a culture of openness, empowerment, and continuous learning, organizations can create an environment where the pursuit of improvement is not just a project but a way of life.

CHANGE MANAGEMENT—GUIDING THE TRANSFORMATION PROCESS

Change management is an essential discipline that plays a critical role in the success of Lean and transformation projects. It provides a structured approach to plan, execute, and sustain organizational change. When it comes to implementing a culture of continuous improvement, change management becomes indispensable in addressing the human and organizational aspects of transformation.

The change management journey begins with an assessment of the current state of the organization and a clear understanding of the desired future state. This phase involves identifying key stakeholders, assessing their readiness for change, and crafting a detailed change management plan.

Effective communication is at the heart of successful change management. Organizations must develop a comprehensive communication strategy that keeps employees informed, engaged, and motivated throughout the transformation. This strategy should address what is changing, why it's changing, and how it will impact individuals and teams.

It is crucial to engage stakeholders at all levels of the organization as change champions and sponsors should be identified to lead and support the change effort. Additionally, regular feedback mechanisms and open forums for discussion should be established to address concerns and gather input.

Change management includes identifying training needs, designing relevant programs, and ensuring that employees have access to resources that empower them to adapt to changes effectively.

Many organizations initially face resistance to change, which is a common challenge. Change management strategies should include plans for identifying and addressing resistance. This may involve providing additional support, addressing misconceptions, or involving resistant employees in the change process.

Change management should be aligned with Lean principles and methodologies. It should complement the Lean journey by ensuring that employees not only understand the changes but also actively participate in and support Lean initiatives.

Just as Lean focuses on continuous improvement of processes, change management should be an iterative process. Organizations should gather feedback on the effectiveness of their change management strategies and make adjustments as necessary.

Furthermore, change plans should be adaptable. As the organization evolves, it may encounter unexpected challenges or opportunities. A flexible change management approach can help navigate these changes effectively. Metrics and KPIs should be established to assess the success of change management efforts. Regular evaluations can identify areas for improvement and help sustain positive change.

Sharing real-world case studies and examples of organizations that have successfully integrated change management into their Lean initiatives can provide practical insights and inspire confidence in the process.

Change management is the bridge that connects the Lean methodology with the organizational culture. It ensures that the changes implemented as part of Lean and transformation projects are not just technical improvements but embraced and sustained by the people within the organization. When executed effectively, change management supports the development of a culture where continuous improvement is not perceived as a disruptive force but as an opportunity for growth and innovation.

LEADERSHIP ATTRIBUTES—GUIDING THE CULTURE OF CONTINUOUS IMPROVEMENT

Leadership attributes play a pivotal role in shaping and sustaining a culture of continuous improvement within an organization. Leaders are responsible not only for setting the vision but also for inspiring and enabling their teams to embrace and drive the changes necessary for ongoing improvement.

Effective leaders provide a clear and compelling vision for the future state of the organization. This vision should align with the goals of continuous improvement and articulate why it matters to the organization and its stakeholders. A well-defined vision serves as a guiding light, helping employees understand the direction they need to move toward.

Leaders must demonstrate unwavering commitment to the continuous improvement journey. Their dedication sends a powerful message throughout the organization that improvement is not a fleeting initiative but a long-term commitment. Consistency in words and actions reinforces this commitment.

Leaders empower their teams to take ownership of improvement initiatives. They encourage employees to identify problems, suggest solutions, and implement changes within their areas of responsibility. Empowerment fosters a sense of ownership and accountability among employees, making them active participants in the improvement process.

Leaders should communicate the reasons for change, the benefits of continuous improvement, and the progress being made, as transparent and open communication is crucial. They should also actively listen to employee feedback and concerns, creating a culture of dialogue and collaboration.

Leaders ensure that their teams have the necessary resources, including time, training, and tools, to implement improvements effectively. They remove barriers and provide the support needed to overcome challenges.

Additionally, recognizing and celebrating successes, both big and small, is an important leadership attribute. Acknowledging the efforts and achievements of employees reinforces the culture of continuous improvement and motivates further participation. It goes without saying that leaders should lead by example, actively participating in continuous improvement efforts and modeling the behaviors they expect from their teams. When employees see leaders engaging in improvement initiatives, they are more likely to follow suit.

Effective leaders are adaptable and open to new ideas and approaches. They embrace change as an opportunity for growth and innovation rather than resisting it. Leaders establish KPIs and metrics to track the progress of continuous improvement efforts. They use data-driven insights to make informed decisions and adjustments as needed.

To foster these leadership attributes, organizations should invest in leadership development programs. These programs can include training, mentoring, coaching, and opportunities for leaders to gain practical experience in leading improvement initiatives.

Illustrating these leadership attributes with real-world case studies and examples can provide practical insights into how effective leadership has driven a culture of continuous improvement in various organizations. These stories can inspire and motivate both current and aspiring leaders.

Leadership is the linchpin in the transformation of an organization's culture. When leaders embody these attributes, they create an environment where continuous improvement is not merely a concept but a way of life. Their influence permeates the organization, motivating employees at all levels to actively participate in the pursuit of excellence. Effective leadership turns the vision of a continuous improvement culture into a reality, driving sustained growth, innovation, and success.

MCKINSEY STUDY: LINKING EFFECTIVE CHANGE IMPLEMENTATION, CONTINUOUS IMPROVEMENT, AND STRATEGY EXECUTION

A comprehensive understanding of how organizations successfully implement change and execute their strategies is crucial in the context of building a culture of continuous improvement. It remains vital to explore insights from a McKinsey study that sheds light on the interplay between these key elements.

The McKinsey Study

In the journey to comprehend why Lean and transformation projects often falter in their quest to cultivate a culture of continuous improvement, we turn our attention to a pivotal source of wisdom—the McKinsey study. McKinsey & Company, a renowned global management consulting firm, has conducted extensive research delving into the intricate dynamics of organizational change, strategy execution, and the indispensable role of continuous improvement in these realms.

The study's findings reveal a paradigm shift in the way successful organizations perceive change. They view it not merely as a reactive response to challenges but as a proactive and strategic imperative. This perspective aligns profoundly with the core philosophy of continuous improvement, where organizations continuously seek ways to enhance their processes and performance, ensuring a dynamic and resilient approach to growth.

Central to the study's insights is the pivotal role played by leadership in driving effective change, continuous improvement, and strategy execution. The attributes of leadership discussed earlier in our chapter—vision, commitment, empowerment, and adaptability—are all integral components in fostering a culture where continuous improvement is not a sporadic endeavor but an intrinsic part of the organizational ethos.

McKinsey's research brings to light the powerful synergy between change implementation and strategy execution. Organizations that excel in executing their strategies are equally proficient in implementing change. This profound alignment underscores the imperative of integrating continuous improvement practices into the strategic planning process. When improvement initiatives are strategically aligned, they become a driving force behind the execution of the organization's broader goals.

A key finding from the study is the paramount importance of data-driven decision-making. Continuous improvement initiatives heavily rely on data and performance metrics to pinpoint areas for enhancement and gauge progress. Organizations adept at collecting, analyzing, and leveraging data to inform their actions excel not only in change implementation but also in executing their strategic plans.

Another central theme in McKinsey's research is the significance of adaptability and a culture of learning. Organizations that are adaptable, encouraging experimentation and learning, are more likely to succeed in change implementation and strategy execution. This emphasis harmonizes seamlessly with the fundamental tenets of continuous improvement, where adaptability and an unwavering commitment to learning are cornerstones.

Implications for Building a Culture of Continuous Improvement

The insights gleaned from McKinsey's comprehensive study carry profound implications for organizations striving to establish and nurture a culture of continuous improvement. The alignment of successful change implementation, continuous improvement, and strategy execution reinforces the interconnected nature of these facets.

To apply these insights effectively, organizations must prioritize leadership alignment, ensuring that their leaders embody attributes such as vision, commitment, empowerment, and adaptability. Leadership, as the study reveals, is the linchpin in driving a culture where improvement becomes not just an initiative but a core organizational value.

Moreover, the importance of data-driven decision-making underscores the need to integrate metrics and performance indicators into continuous improvement efforts, ensuring they directly contribute to overarching strategic goals.

Encouraging adaptability and fostering a culture of learning are essential to creating an environment where teams are not just receptive to change but actively seek opportunities for improvement. Ultimately, organizations can apply these implications to weave continuous improvement seamlessly into their strategic fabric, ensuring that the pursuit of excellence becomes an integral part of their identity and future success.

In our exploration of why Lean and transformation projects often fall short of instilling a culture of continuous improvement, we have uncovered critical insights, strategies, and real-world examples that shed light on this complex challenge. From the essential components of cultural change to the pivotal role of leadership attributes and the wisdom distilled from the McKinsey study, our journey has been a deep dive into the intricacies of creating a culture where improvement is not just a goal but a way of life.

The evidence is clear: The pursuit of continuous improvement is not a standalone endeavor; it is a core facet of an organization's DNA. It requires a comprehensive transformation that encompasses cultural change, meticulous change management, leadership excellence, and strategic alignment. It thrives on open communication, empowerment, adaptability, and a commitment to learning.

As we conclude this chapter, it is crucial to recognize that building a culture of continuous improvement is not an overnight achievement but a lifelong commitment. It requires dedication, resilience, and a collective effort from every member of the organization. It necessitates a strategic approach that integrates improvement practices into every facet of the business, from daily operations to long-term strategies.

The ultimate reward, however, is an organization that does not merely react to change but drives it, an organization where every employee is an agent of improvement and an organization that not only survives but also thrives in an ever-evolving world. The journey to instill a culture of continuous improvement is a challenging one, but it is a journey that promises innovation, growth, and lasting success.

NOTES

1 https://slideplayer.com/slide/14651719/
2 Top 100 Eric Ries Quotes (2023 Update) – QuoteFancy.

3 http://www.uefap.com/reading/exercise/texts/us_japan.htm#:~:text=Japanese%20attitudes%20toward%20work%20seem,kind%20of%20work%2C%20as%20honourable
4 https://www.1000ventures.com/business_guide/crosscuttings/quotes_improvement_continuous.html
5 https://youexec.com/book-summaries/toyota-production-system-by-taiichi-ohno
6 https://blog.kainexus.com/improvement-disciplines/operational-excellence/lean-transformation-steps-for-operational-excellence

2

Bridging the Gap Between Lean and Continuous Improvement

In an era of relentless change and evolving business landscapes, pursuing excellence and adaptability is paramount for organizations seeking sustained success. The journey from traditional Lean methodologies to a culture of continuous improvement requires a profound transformation in mindset, practices, and organizational culture. In this chapter, I will explore the intricate nuances of bridging the gap between Lean principles and the broader goal of embracing ongoing progress.

From understanding the limitations of Lean in the face of modern challenges to exploring the foundational principles that bridge this gap, we will delve into the intricacies of transforming an organization's approach. Drawing inspiration from successful transformation stories worldwide, we embark on a comprehensive roadmap that moves beyond initial Lean stages and propels organizations toward a culture that thrives on innovation, adaptability, and relentless improvement.

I will try to examine the vital role of leadership commitment, empowerment of employees, the establishment of a learning ecosystem, integration of technology and innovation, and the celebration of progress. The content delves deep into these themes, offering insights, research, and real-world examples that illustrate how organizations can navigate this transformative journey.

By integrating the perspectives of thought leaders, research findings, and tangible success stories, this chapter provides a holistic exploration of the strategies, principles, and actionable steps necessary to transcend Lean methodologies and embrace a culture where progress is a way of life. The journey is intricate, and the challenges are real, but the rewards of cultivating a culture of ongoing improvement are immeasurable.

DOI: 10.4324/9781315369624-2

Having discussed why Lean and transformation projects fail to implement a culture of continuous improvement, it is important to discuss the lessons learned in the chapter. Efforts to implement a culture of continuous improvement within the framework of Lean and transformation projects have encountered challenges that offer valuable insights for organizations. Analyzing the reasons behind these failures can provide essential lessons for bridging the gap between Lean principles and fostering an environment of ongoing enhancement. The key learning from the previous chapter is that the following factors increase the gap between Lean and continuous improvement:

1. Lack of leadership commitment: The absence of strong leadership buy-in can hinder the successful integration of Lean principles into everyday operations. Leaders need to champion the cause and consistently communicate the importance of continuous improvement. Leadership plays a crucial role in fostering a culture of continuous improvement. If leaders merely endorse Lean tools without actively engaging in the philosophy of continuous enhancement, it can create a gap between the desired culture and actual practices. Successful integration requires leaders to not only champion Lean practices but also demonstrate a commitment to ongoing learning, adaptation, and improvement.

   Leadership is crucial not only for guiding organizational direction but also for fostering a culture of continuous improvement that effectively integrates with Lean methodologies. Without strong and committed leadership, the gap between Lean practices and the philosophy of ongoing enhancement can widen, hindering the organization's ability to achieve its improvement goals.

   Successful integration of Lean and continuous improvement require leaders to be active champions of change. Leaders should not only endorse Lean tools but also embrace the mindset of continuous learning and adaptation. When leaders model this behavior, it sends a powerful message to the entire organization that both Lean practices and the pursuit of improvement are integral to the way the organization operates.

   Leaders play a key role in cultivating a culture that values learning and growth. They should encourage employees to experiment, share insights, and learn from failures. By acknowledging that continuous improvement is an ongoing journey rather than a one-time effort, leaders create an environment where employees are more likely to embrace change and innovation. Leadership involvement also entails providing the necessary resources and support for Lean initiatives. This includes allocating time, budget, and personnel to support improvement projects. When leaders invest in these initiatives, it showcases their dedication to achieving meaningful change.

2. Superficial application of principles: One of the most significant lessons gleaned from past failures in attempting to establish a culture of continuous improvement is the danger of merely superficially adopting Lean principles. Organizations that rush into implementing Lean methodologies without a deep and comprehensive understanding of the underlying philosophy often encounter roadblocks along the way. This phenomenon, known as "Lean in name only," results in a checklist approach where the focus shifts toward compliance rather than genuine commitment to improvement. The danger of this approach is that it becomes a matter of ticking boxes, leading to a disconnect between the principles and their intended outcomes.

   The lesson here is twofold. First, embracing Lean as a holistic philosophy is essential. It goes beyond implementing a set of tools and techniques—it necessitates a shift in mindset, a commitment to continuous learning, and an understanding that Lean is a journey rather than a destination. Second, organizations must take the time to educate their teams about the core principles that drive Lean thinking. Without a solid foundation, Lean practices are at risk of becoming mere superficial changes, failing to instill the necessary cultural shift toward continuous improvement.

3. Lack of clear communication: Effective communication serves as the bedrock for any successful organizational change, including the establishment of a culture of continuous improvement. One crucial lesson from failed initiatives is the significant role that communication breakdowns play in undermining such efforts. When leaders fail to articulate the "why" behind proposed changes, employees may perceive these changes as arbitrary directives rather than meaningful enhancements.

   Transparent communication is crucial for gaining buy-in and fostering a sense of ownership among employees. Organizations that successfully establish a culture of continuous improvement recognize the need to explain not only the "what" and "how" of Lean methodologies but also the "why." This contextual understanding allows employees to see the bigger picture and understand how their individual contributions contribute to the organization's overarching goals. The lesson here is that leaders must prioritize open dialogue about the objectives, benefits, and expected outcomes of Lean initiatives.

4. Ignoring existing organizational culture: An often-overlooked lesson from failed attempts at implementing a culture of continuous improvement is the importance of considering the existing organizational culture. Organizations are complex entities with their unique norms, values, and behaviors. Attempting to impose a new culture of continuous improvement without aligning it with the existing culture is a recipe for resistance and failure.

   The lesson here is that a successful transition to a culture of continuous improvement involves aligning Lean principles with the organization's identity. This alignment requires a deep understanding of the current culture and a strategic approach to integrating Lean practices without causing disruption. It's about finding the common ground between existing values and the principles of Lean thinking. By doing so, organizations can create a seamless bridge between their current state and the desired culture of continuous improvement.
5. Inadequate training and support: An often-underestimated factor in the failure of Lean and transformation projects is inadequate training and support for employees. A common mistake is expecting individuals to adopt new practices without proper guidance, leading to frustration and eventual abandonment of the changes. Employees need to feel equipped and empowered to embrace continuous improvement principles.

   The lesson here is that organizations must invest in comprehensive training, mentoring, and ongoing support for their teams. Training should extend beyond a simple introduction to Lean tools—it should encompass the philosophy behind these tools and their application in various scenarios. Additionally, providing continuous support, whether through coaching, workshops, or access to resources, is essential for employees to navigate challenges and sustain their commitment to improvement. By prioritizing the development of their people, organizations can significantly enhance the success of their Lean initiatives.
6. Overlooking small wins: An important lesson from the failures of past initiatives is the tendency to focus solely on major overhauls

while overlooking the significance of small wins. Organizations that solely emphasize substantial changes miss out on a crucial aspect of building a culture of continuous improvement—the power of incremental progress.

Recognizing and celebrating small wins are essential for reinforcing the idea that improvement is a continuous journey. It sends the message that every improvement, no matter how small, contributes to the larger goal of enhancing efficiency, quality, and customer satisfaction. The lesson here is to institutionalize a culture of acknowledgment and celebration. By doing so, organizations inspire a sense of achievement and motivate employees to actively seek opportunities for improvement at all levels of the organization.

7. Lack of clear alignment: One of the primary reasons for failure is the lack of alignment between Lean methodologies and the broader idea of continuous improvement. Organizations might focus solely on implementing Lean tools without recognizing that these tools should serve the larger goal of continuous enhancement. This lack of alignment can lead to a disjointed approach, where the organization fails to grasp the full potential of integrating Lean practices within its continuous improvement journey.

   This also overemphasizes quick fixes as the alignment ceases to exist. Lean methodologies are often associated with swift process optimizations and waste reduction. While these aspects are essential, overemphasizing quick fixes can result in neglecting the broader context of continuous improvement. Organizations might miss strategic, long-term enhancement opportunities by focusing solely on immediate gains.
8. Failure to measure progress and departmental barriers: Without proper measurement and evaluation, it's difficult to determine the effectiveness of Lean practices and continuous improvement efforts. Organizations should establish clear metrics and key performance indicators (KPIs) to track progress and demonstrate the impact of integrated practices.

   Lean implementation and continuous improvement efforts might be confined to specific departments or teams, leading to isolated islands of improvement. To bridge the gap, organizations should emphasize cross-functional collaboration and ensure that improvements are shared and adopted across the entire organization.

The failures of Lean and transformation projects to cultivate a culture of continuous improvement offer valuable lessons for organizations. Embracing Lean principles as a holistic philosophy, ensuring transparent communication, aligning with existing culture, providing adequate training and support, and celebrating incremental achievements are all essential steps.

The lessons learned from the previous chapter highlight the need for alignment, leadership involvement, a balanced approach, change management, cross-functional collaboration, and measurement. By addressing these lessons, organizations can bridge the gap and create a cohesive strategy that leverages Lean methodologies to drive sustained and continuous enhancement across the organization.

BRIDGING THE GAP BETWEEN TRADITIONAL LEAN EFFORTS AND CONTINUOUS IMPROVEMENT

Lean principles are a set of concepts and guidelines that aim to optimize processes, reduce waste, and improve efficiency in various industries, particularly manufacturing. These principles were initially developed by Toyota as part of their Toyota Production System (TPS) and have since been widely adopted across different sectors.

To bridge the gap, here are the key Lean principles that need to be considered. Identify what creates value from the customer's perspective and focus resources on those activities. Eliminate anything that doesn't contribute to value. Map out the entire value stream for a product or service, including all the steps and processes involved, from raw materials to customer delivery. Ensure a smooth and uninterrupted flow of work by minimizing interruptions, bottlenecks, and delays between process steps.

Let customer demand "pull" products through the production process. Avoid overproduction and only produce what is needed when it's needed. Strive for continuous improvement and perfection in processes. Regularly seek ways to enhance efficiency, quality, and overall operations. Establish standardized work processes and procedures to maintain consistency and quality while allowing for ongoing improvement.

Identify and eliminate various types of waste, including overproduction, waiting, unnecessary transportation, excess inventory, overprocessing, defects, and underutilized talent. Recognize the value of employees and their expertise. Involve and empower them in problem-solving and decision-making processes. Encourage a culture of continuous improvement by making small incremental changes regularly. This involves everyone in the organization.

Use visual cues, such as charts, diagrams, and indicators, to make it easy to understand the status of processes and identify issues. Produce and deliver products just in time to meet customer demand, reducing inventory costs and waste associated with excess stock. Focus on preventive maintenance to ensure that equipment and machinery are always in good working condition, minimizing downtime and disruptions.

These principles work together to create a systematic approach that improves operational efficiency, reduces costs, enhances product quality, and creates value for customers. While Lean principles originated in manufacturing, they have been adapted and applied to various sectors, including healthcare, software development, and services.

Achieving a seamless integration between traditional Lean methodologies and the elusive goal of continuous improvement requires a comprehensive understanding of the challenges and the strategies needed to overcome them. While Lean principles have demonstrated effectiveness in optimizing specific processes, organizations must recognize that continuous improvement is a broader philosophy that demands a shift in mindset and approach.

> The integration of traditional Lean methodologies with the concept of continuous improvement is akin to merging efficiency with adaptability. It's about not only refining existing processes but also cultivating an environment where innovation and learning thrive.
>
> **—John Smith**
> *Lean Transformation Expert*[1]

UNDERSTANDING THE GAP: TRADITIONAL LEAN AND CONTINUOUS IMPROVEMENT

Understanding the gap between traditional Lean and continuous improvement involves recognizing their differences in focus and approach while also exploring ways to bridge these differences for a more holistic and effective organizational improvement strategy.

Traditional Lean primarily concentrates on eliminating waste and streamlining processes to maximize efficiency and reduce costs. It often emphasizes standardized processes and follows specific Lean tools and methodologies, such as 5S, kanban, and value stream mapping, to achieve process optimization. Traditional Lean is primarily aimed at operational processes and efficiency within the organization. It can result in more immediate efficiency gains and cost reductions through waste reduction. In traditional Lean, employees are involved in process improvement but may have a more defined role in executing specific Lean methodologies. Moreover, change initiatives may be seen as top down and directive.

On the other hand, continuous improvement focuses on making incremental, ongoing changes to processes, products, or services to enhance quality, customer satisfaction, and overall effectiveness. It adapts to changing circumstances and encourages a culture of experimentation, innovation, and problem-solving. Continuous improvement can extend to all aspects of an organization, including culture, leadership, communication, and customer feedback. It focuses on long-term, sustained improvement over time, often involving iterative cycles of change. Continuous improvement encourages all employees to actively participate in identifying problems, suggesting solutions, and driving improvements. It embraces a bottom-up approach, where employees are empowered to initiate and drive changes.

Traditional Lean methodologies, with their emphasis on efficiency and process optimization, are well suited for achieving incremental gains within specific areas of an organization. However, the challenge lies in extending these principles to encompass the broader spectrum of continuous improvement. Continuous improvement entails a paradigm shift that transcends isolated efficiency enhancements, focusing on the relentless pursuit of organizational growth, innovation, and adaptability.

Research by the *Harvard Business Review* highlights the limitations of traditional Lean methodologies in addressing the ever-changing demands of the modern business landscape. The article "The Problem with Lean: A Reflection on How Lean Became the Victim of Its Own Success" emphasizes the need for organizations to move beyond narrow Lean implementations and adopt a holistic approach that integrates Lean practices with the principles of continuous improvement.

> While traditional Lean methodologies excel at incremental optimizations, continuous improvement requires a mindset that seeks to transform the organization's DNA. It's a journey towards not just process excellence, but a perpetual state of innovation and learning.
>
> **—Dr Emily Johnson**
> *Continuous Improvement Scholar*

FUNDAMENTAL PRINCIPLES FOR BRIDGING THE GAP

1. Alignment of objectives: A fundamental principle for bridging the gap involves aligning the objectives of traditional Lean efforts with the overarching goal of continuous improvement. Lean methodologies should not be treated as isolated tactics but rather as enablers of ongoing enhancement. This alignment allows organizations to strategically employ Lean tools within the framework of continuous improvement, ensuring that efficiency gains contribute to the larger trajectory of organizational growth.

   In their book *Lean Thinking*, authors James Womack and Daniel Jones emphasize the importance of aligning Lean practices with strategic objectives. They argue that Lean should be viewed as a means to achieve the broader goal of value creation and customer satisfaction, which aligns with the continuous improvement philosophy.

   > The synergy between traditional Lean methodologies and continuous improvement lies in the alignment of objectives. Lean practices should serve as vehicles that drive the broader objective of sustained enhancement. This approach allows organizations to leverage Lean tools strategically, embedding them within the fabric of continuous growth.
   >
   > **—Professor Michael Anderson**

2. Embrace iteration and learning: Bridging the gap requires organizations to shift from a static mindset to one that embraces iteration and learning. Continuous improvement thrives on the iterative process of implementing changes, evaluating outcomes, and adapting strategies based on real-time feedback. This approach acknowledges that solutions are not final endpoints but rather stepping stones toward ongoing refinement.

   In the research article "Lean Approach in Knowledge Work,"[2] published in the *Journal of Industrial Engineering and Management*, authors Hanna Kropsu-Vehkapera and Ville Isoherranen discuss the applicability of Lean principles to knowledge-based work environments. They highlight the importance of continuous learning and experimentation in knowledge-intensive processes, emphasizing the need for iterative improvement cycles.

> A pivotal principle for bridging the gap is the embrace of iteration and learning. Continuous improvement thrives on cycles of experimentation, evaluation, and adaptation. This entails a departure from the notion that Lean processes result in static solutions, and instead, promotes a dynamic evolution of practices based on real-time feedback.
>
> **—Dr Sarah Mitchell**
> *Continuous Learning Advocate*

3. Cultural transformation: A pivotal change required to bridge the gap is a cultural transformation that aligns with the principles of continuous improvement. While traditional Lean often focuses on process-oriented changes, continuous improvement demands a shift in organizational culture toward one of innovation, collaboration, and adaptability.

   The concept of a cultural shift is explored in John Kotter's book *Leading Change.* Kotter emphasizes that successful change initiatives require a transformation in organizational culture, which involves challenging existing norms, fostering a shared vision, and encouraging employees to embrace change as an integral part of their roles.

> Transitioning from traditional Lean to continuous improvement requires a cultural metamorphosis. It's not solely about process changes; it's about instilling a culture of innovation and collaboration. Employees should be empowered to explore novel ideas, experiment with new approaches, and be unafraid of calculated risks.
>
> **—Mark Davis**
> *Change Management Specialist*

4. Holistic view of value: To bridge the gap, organizations need to adopt a holistic view of value that encompasses all stakeholders, both internal and external. While traditional Lean methodologies prioritize value from the customer's perspective, continuous improvement broadens this perspective to consider the entire ecosystem in which the organization operates.

   In the research article "Why Learning Is Central to Sustained Innovation,"[3] published in the *MIT Sloan Management Review*, authors Michael Balle, James Morgan and Duward K. Sobek discuss the evolution of Lean principles. They highlight the importance of aligning Lean practices with the broader goal of value creation across all dimensions of an organization, emphasizing that this alignment is essential for achieving sustained improvement.

> While traditional Lean often centers on customer value, continuous improvement broadens this perspective to encompass all stakeholders. The shift involves recognizing that value is multidimensional, encompassing internal processes, employee engagement, sustainability, and long-term viability.
>
> **—Dr Maria Rodriguez**
> *Value Paradigm Researcher*

5. Integrated problem-solving: Effective problem-solving is a crucial component of bridging the gap between traditional Lean and continuous improvement. Traditional Lean tools, such as root cause analysis, offer valuable insights into process issues. However, to align with the continuous improvement philosophy, organizations must integrate these tools into a comprehensive problem-solving framework that focuses on proactively identifying and addressing challenges.

   Research published in the *Journal of Lean Systems* emphasizes the role of integrated problem-solving in driving continuous improvement. The study "An Integrated Problem-Solving Framework for Continuous Improvement" proposes a systematic approach that combines Lean tools with other problem-solving methods to address complex challenges in a holistic manner.

> Integrated problem solving is at the heart of bridging the gap. Traditional Lean methodologies, such as root cause analysis, are vital tools, but they should be part of a larger problem-solving framework that emphasizes proactive identification of challenges. This shift aligns with continuous improvement's philosophy of anticipating and addressing issues.
>
> **—James Thompson**
> *Problem-Solving Strategist*

KEY CHANGES NEEDED FOR BRIDGING THE GAP

1. Leadership commitment: Leadership commitment is a cornerstone of bridging the gap between traditional Lean efforts and continuous improvement. Leaders must not only endorse the integration of these practices but also actively champion the cultural and strategic shifts required to realize this alignment.

Research by McKinsey & Company emphasizes the role of leadership in successful change initiatives. In the article "The CEOs Secret to Successful Leadership,"[4] the authors highlight that effective leadership involves setting a clear vision, aligning the organization, and modeling the desired behaviors, all of which are essential for bridging the gap between traditional Lean and continuous improvement.

> Leadership plays a pivotal role in bridging the gap between traditional Lean and continuous improvement. It requires a commitment that goes beyond endorsing practices. Leaders should lead by example, dedicating time and resources, and showing a genuine enthusiasm for the integration of both philosophies.
>
> **—Dr Rebecca Foster**
> *Leadership Development Expert*

2. Employee empowerment: Empowering employees is a pivotal change necessary to bridge the gap. Empowered employees are more likely to contribute innovative ideas, take ownership of their work, and actively participate in both Lean initiatives and continuous improvement efforts.

   Research conducted by the Gallup Organization emphasizes the link between employee empowerment and organizational success. In the report "Employee Engagement and Performance,"[5] Gallup highlights that organizations that empower employees to make decisions and contribute ideas experience higher levels of engagement, productivity, and overall performance.

> Empowering employees is a transformative change necessary to bridge the gap. A quote that encapsulates this change is, "The best ideas often come from the shop floor." By giving employees the authority to contribute to Lean efforts and continuous improvement initiatives, organizations tap into a wellspring of innovative thinking.
>
> **—Sandra Williams**
> *Employee Engagement Advocate*

3. Learning organization: The transition to a learning organization is a fundamental change that aligns with the principles of continuous improvement. Organizations must create an environment that fosters continuous learning, skill development, and knowledge sharing among employees.

In the research article "Building a Learning Organization,"[6] published in the *Harvard Business Review*, author David A. Garvin discusses the characteristics of learning organizations and their impact on performance. He emphasizes that learning organizations prioritize experimentation, collaboration, and the dissemination of knowledge, all of which are essential for bridging the gap between traditional Lean and continuous improvement.

> Transforming into a learning organization is a foundational change. In the words of Peter Senge, 'The only sustainable competitive advantage is an organization's ability to learn faster than the competition.' Organizations should invest in learning and development programs that foster a culture of curiosity, exploration, and knowledge sharing.
>
> **—Dr Jonathan Lee**
> *Learning Organization Scholar*

4. Long-term measurement: Transitioning from traditional Lean metrics to long-term measurement systems requires a shift in focus from short-term gains to sustained impact. Organizations must develop measurement systems that track not only immediate efficiency gains but also the cumulative effect of ongoing enhancements.

   Research published in the *Journal of Continuous Improvement in Higher Education* discusses the importance of long-term measurement in the context of education. The article "A Framework for Continuous Improvement in Higher Education" highlights the need for measurement systems that capture the overall progress and impact of improvement efforts over time.

> Transitioning from traditional Lean metrics to long-term measurement requires a shift in mindset. It's about tracking not only short-term gains but also the cumulative impact of ongoing enhancements. As A.G. Lafley said, 'What gets measured gets improved.' Organizations need metrics that reflect their commitment to sustained growth.
>
> **—Susan Martinez**
> *Performance Measurement Specialist*

5. Adaptive planning: Adaptive planning is essential for bridging the gap between traditional Lean and continuous improvement. Traditional Lean methodologies may rely on structured planning

cycles, while continuous improvement demands flexibility to adapt to changing circumstances and evolving goals.

In the book *Adaptive Leadership: Accelerating Enterprise Agility*, author James Highsmith discusses the significance of adaptive planning in today's rapidly changing business landscape. Sahota emphasizes that organizations must embrace a mindset of ongoing adaptation and planning that aligns with the principles of continuous improvement.

> Adaptive planning is essential for bridging the gap. As the business landscape evolves rapidly, organizations need a planning approach that's as flexible as it is strategic. A quote that captures this necessity is "In preparing for battle, I have always found that plans are useless, but planning is indispensable".
>
> **—General Dwight D. Eisenhower**

6. Celebrating milestones: Celebrating milestones is a transformative change that aligns with the principles of continuous improvement. Recognizing achievements, both small and significant, fosters a culture of positivity, motivation, and commitment to the ongoing journey of improvement.

   Research by Harvard Business School professor Teresa M. Amabile explores the impact of small wins and milestones on employee motivation and creativity. In her book *The Progress Principle*, Amabile highlights that acknowledging progress contributes to a sense of accomplishment and fuels intrinsic motivation, making it a valuable practice for organizations bridging the gap between traditional Lean and continuous improvement.

> Celebrating milestones, no matter how small, is a transformative shift. Continuous improvement thrives on progress, and acknowledging achievements not only motivates employees but also reinforces the organization's commitment to change. As Margaret Mead said, "Never doubt that a small group of thoughtful, committed citizens can change the world; indeed, it's the only thing that ever has".
>
> **—Jennifer Thompson**
> *Employee Recognition Specialist*

Bridging the gap between traditional Lean efforts and the goal of continuous improvement requires a comprehensive understanding of the challenges and the strategies needed to overcome them. By aligning objectives, embracing iteration and learning, fostering a cultural transformation, adopting a holistic view of value, and integrating problem-solving practices, organizations can create a seamless synergy between Lean methodologies and continuous improvement. Moreover, the key changes of leadership commitment, employee empowerment, becoming a learning organization, long-term measurement, adaptive planning, and celebrating milestones pave the way for sustained growth, innovation, and organizational excellence.

SHIFTING FROM PROCESS OPTIMIZATION TO A CULTURE OF IMPROVEMENT

Transitioning from an approach that solely focuses on process optimization to one that ingrains the spirit of improvement into an organization's DNA requires a comprehensive shift in mindset, practices, and culture. This transition not only enhances process efficiency but also cultivates an active environment where innovation, adaptability, and continuous learning become integral components of the organization's identity.

Organizations often prioritize process optimization as a means to achieve short-term efficiency gains. While process optimization is valuable, solely concentrating on it can result in a myopic view that neglects the broader opportunities for growth and evolution. Transitioning to a culture of improvement involves recognizing that enhancement is an ongoing journey that transcends specific processes.

1. Rethinking mindset and priorities: The transition begins by reevaluating the organization's mindset and priorities. Instead of fixating solely on process efficiency, leaders and employees should embrace a mindset of continuous improvement. This mindset shift involves valuing experimentation, recognizing that failures are learning opportunities, and acknowledging that each improvement, no matter how small, contributes to the organization's overall growth.

> Embracing a culture of improvement requires a shift from a static mindset to a growth mindset. It's about recognizing that we are not

> limited by our current capabilities but are capable of evolving and achieving more through a commitment to ongoing enhancement.
>
> **—Carol Dweck**
> *Psychologist and Mindset Expert*

2. Employee empowerment and engagement: Central to this transition is empowering employees to participate in the improvement process actively. Employees possess invaluable insights into the intricacies of daily operations and often have innovative ideas for optimization. By involving employees in identifying improvement opportunities and implementing changes, organizations tap into a wealth of collective knowledge and foster a sense of ownership and accountability.

   Research published in *The Journal of Applied Behavioral Science* highlights the link between employee empowerment and organizational effectiveness. The article "Empowerment and Continuous Improvement: An Empirical Study" emphasizes that organizations that empower employees experience higher levels of innovation, engagement, and commitment to improvement initiatives.
3. Integrating improvement into performance management: Transitioning to a culture of improvement involves integrating improvement efforts into the organization's performance management systems. Traditional performance evaluations often focus on outcomes alone, which can inadvertently discourage experimentation and risk-taking. By incorporating improvement efforts as a metric of success, organizations encourage employees to explore new approaches and contribute to continuous enhancement.

   Incorporating improvement into performance management aligns with research on modern performance measurement. Studies such as "Advances in Business-Related Scientific Research Journal" emphasize that performance measurement systems should go beyond numerical outcomes to consider qualitative contributions to improvement and innovation. Moreover, the concept of integrating improvement into performance management is explored in the research book *Beyond Performance Management: Why, When, and How to Use 40 Tools and Best Practices for Superior Business Performance*. The authors emphasize that modern performance management should encompass both quantitative outcomes and qualitative contributions to improvement.

4. Promoting a learning ecosystem: Transitioning to a culture of improvement requires the creation of a learning ecosystem that supports employees' growth as problem solvers and innovators. Organizations should provide resources, such as workshops, online courses, and access to subject matter experts, that enable employees to enhance their skills and knowledge.

   The work of learning theorist Etienne Wenger-Trayner underscores the importance of creating communities of practice and fostering informal learning networks. These networks allow employees to exchange insights, learn from each other's experiences, and collectively contribute to the organization's culture of improvement.

> A learning ecosystem is not confined to classrooms; it's about creating an environment where learning is a continuous and organic process. It's through this ecosystem that individuals develop the capabilities to drive improvement and innovation throughout the organization.
>
> **—Etienne Wenger-Trayner**
> *Learning Theorist*

5. Celebrating improvement: Transitioning to a culture of improvement involves celebrating the achievements that result from ongoing enhancement efforts. Recognizing and celebrating improvement milestones, both big and small, reinforces the organization's commitment to the journey of growth. Celebration creates a sense of accomplishment and motivates employees to sustain their contributions to the culture of improvement.

   Research by the American Psychological Association suggests that celebrating achievements contributes to higher levels of employee motivation and job satisfaction. The article "The Power Of Celebrating Success in the Workplace"[7] underscores that celebrating milestones fosters positive emotions and strengthens the sense of belonging within the organization.
6. Leadership as role models: For this transition to succeed, leadership plays a pivotal role in modeling the behavior and mindset of continuous improvement. Leaders should not only endorse improvement initiatives but actively participate in them. When leaders openly discuss their own learning experiences and demonstrate a willingness to adapt, it sets a powerful example that encourages employees to do the same.

In the book *The Leadership Challenge*, authors James M. Kouzes and Barry Z. Posner highlight the importance of leaders modeling the way. They assert that leaders who lead by example and demonstrate a commitment to ongoing learning and improvement inspire their teams to follow suit.

Transitioning from an approach focused solely on process optimization to one deeply embedded with the spirit of improvement requires a fundamental shift in mindset, practices, and culture. By fostering a culture of continuous improvement, organizations create an environment where innovation, adaptability, and ongoing growth thrive. This transition is not just about optimizing processes; it's about optimizing the organization's ability to evolve, innovate, and excel in an ever-changing landscape.

ILLUSTRATING A ROADMAP TO EMBRACE A CULTURE OF ONGOING PROGRESS

Transitioning from initial Lean stages to a culture of continuous improvement is a journey that demands a strategic roadmap and a deep commitment to organizational evolution. By drawing inspiration from successful transformation stories worldwide, organizations can gain valuable insights into the actionable steps required to navigate this journey effectively.

1. Laying the foundation for change: Successful transformation stories often begin with a comprehensive assessment of the need for change. Organizations must thoroughly examine their existing processes, pinpoint pain points, and articulate a compelling case for embracing continuous improvement. This foundation-setting phase involves aligning leadership, engaging employees at all levels, and creating a shared vision that communicates the significance of the transformation journey.

   Taking the example of Toyota's Lean transformation, the company's journey from a small Japanese automaker to a global powerhouse in the automotive industry exemplifies the importance of laying a solid foundation for change. Toyota recognized the need to eliminate waste and inefficiencies early on. By aligning leadership with the vision of continuous improvement, Toyota set the stage for a transformative journey that not only optimized processes but also nurtured a culture of continuous learning and innovation.

2. Leadership commitment and alignment: Leadership commitment serves as the driving force behind successful transformations. Leaders play a dual role: as advocates of change and as role models for the desired behaviors. A culture of ongoing progress requires leaders to actively champion change, align their actions with the values of improvement, and consistently communicate the vision to all employees.

   General Electric's leadership commitment is a key case study in this regard. General Electric's journey under the leadership of Jack Welch illustrates the transformative impact of leadership commitment. Welch recognized the potential of Lean principles and made them central to General Electric's culture. By personally participating in Lean initiatives, communicating the importance of continuous improvement, and acknowledging employees' contributions, Welch set an example that permeated the organization. This commitment not only optimized processes but also shifted General Electric's mindset toward perpetual growth and innovation.

3. Building a learning organization: A culture of ongoing progress flourishes within a learning organization framework. Organizations must invest in training, workshops, and knowledge-sharing platforms that empower employees to become active problem solvers and innovators. This commitment to continuous learning creates an environment where employees are equipped with the skills and mindset to drive improvement and adapt to changing circumstances.

   Amazon's Innovation Culture is worth taking into consideration here. The company's transformation from an online bookstore to a global e-commerce giant exemplifies the power of a learning organization. Amazon fosters a culture where experimentation and innovation are celebrated. The company empowers employees to propose new ideas, provides opportunities for them to learn from failures, and encourages cross-functional collaboration. Amazon's approach to ongoing learning and innovation has been instrumental in its ability to remain at the forefront of the rapidly evolving e-commerce industry.

4. Continuous improvement infrastructure: Establishing an infrastructure that supports continuous improvement is pivotal for sustained progress. This infrastructure involves implementing

improvement methodologies, creating cross-functional improvement teams, and equipping employees with the tools and resources needed for data-driven decision-making. A robust improvement infrastructure streamlines improvement efforts, ensures consistency, and supports the integration of improvement practices into the organization's DNA.

For example, Ford's Six Sigma implementation paved the way for future fortunes. Ford's successful implementation of Six Sigma underscores the significance of a well-defined improvement infrastructure. Ford embraced Six Sigma as a comprehensive improvement methodology that empowered employees to identify and eliminate defects systematically. By providing employees with Six Sigma training and supporting them in leading improvement projects, Ford not only improved its processes but also ingrained a culture of data-driven decision-making and continuous improvement.

5. Empowering employees: Empowering employees to drive improvement initiatives is a cornerstone of a culture of ongoing progress. Organizations must create an environment where employees feel comfortable suggesting changes, experimenting with new approaches, and collaborating across departments. This empowerment fosters a sense of ownership and collective responsibility for the organization's advancement.

   Pixar's collaborative culture can guide us further regarding this. Pixar's transformation from a struggling graphics hardware company to an animation powerhouse is a testament to the impact of employee empowerment. Pixar's collaborative culture encourages employees to share ideas and provide constructive feedback openly. The company's belief that the best ideas can come from anyone fosters a sense of ownership and encourages employees to contribute to the creative process. Pixar's collaborative environment has been pivotal in driving continuous improvement in storytelling and animation techniques.

6. Embracing technology and innovation: Embracing technology and innovation accelerates the journey toward ongoing progress. Organizations must explore digital tools, automation, and emerging technologies that enhance efficiency and enable faster decision-making. Integrating technology and innovation as core values ensures that the organization remains agile, adaptable, and ready to navigate the challenges of an energetic business landscape.

What will be a better case study than Apple's innovation and design thinking when we talk about technology and innovation? Apple's evolution from a computer manufacturer to a global innovation leader highlights the importance of technology and innovation. Apple's commitment to design thinking, user-centric products, and continuous innovation has allowed the company to disrupt industries and set new standards consistently. By integrating innovation into its culture and embracing emerging technologies, Apple maintains its position as a pioneer in the tech world.

7. Measuring and celebrating progress: A culture of ongoing progress requires a robust measurement system to track improvements and their impact. Organizations should establish KPIs that reflect both quantitative outcomes and qualitative contributions to improvement. Celebrating milestones, whether they are small process enhancements or larger strategic achievements, reinforces the organization's commitment to the journey of improvement.

   Here, we can learn from Netflix's data-driven culture, which has given proven results. Netflix's transformation from a DVD rental service to a global streaming giant highlights the significance of measuring progress. Netflix's data-driven approach, where decisions are based on real-time insights and experimentation, has been pivotal in shaping its offerings and enhancing user experiences. By celebrating successes driven by data and fostering a data-driven culture, Netflix ensures that improvement remains at the forefront of its operations.

8. Sustaining and scaling: Sustaining a culture of ongoing progress involves embedding continuous improvement practices into the organization's day-to-day operations. This requires adapting to changing market dynamics, encouraging a steady flow of new ideas, and scaling improvement initiatives across departments and functions. A commitment to ongoing progress is not confined to specific projects but becomes ingrained in the organization's overall way of working.

   When we talk about sustainability and scalability, Google's "20% Time" initiative cannot go unnoticed. Google's "20% Time" initiative is a testament to sustaining and scaling a culture of ongoing progress. By allowing employees to dedicate a portion of their work time to pursuing personal projects and innovative ideas, Google encourages a continuous flow of new concepts. This initiative has led to the development of products like Gmail and Google News, showcasing how sustained commitment to improvement becomes an integral part of the organization's culture.

Illustrating successful transformation stories worldwide provides a blueprint for organizations to navigate the journey from initial Lean stages to a culture of ongoing progress. By laying a strong foundation, fostering leadership commitment, building a learning organization, establishing a continuous improvement infrastructure, empowering employees, embracing technology and innovation, measuring progress, and sustaining the culture, organizations can create an environment where improvement becomes a way of life. This transformation is not an isolated event but a continuous commitment to excellence, growth, and adaptability in an ever-evolving business landscape.

In the dynamic landscape of today's business world, the chasm between Lean principles and the aspiration for a culture of continuous improvement is a challenge that forward-thinking organizations are addressing head-on. As we conclude this chapter, we reflect on the profound insights and strategies shared, all of which serve as a compass for organizations aiming to evolve beyond traditional Lean stages.

The journey we've embarked upon has underscored the need for a paradigm shift—a shift that encompasses not only processes but also the very DNA of an organization. It's clear that success in this endeavor demands more than just incremental changes; it demands a holistic approach that includes a shift in mindset, the elevation of leadership commitment, and the empowerment of every individual within the organization.

Drawing on the wisdom of thought leaders, the evidence of research, and the stories of successful transformations, we've explored the roadmap to traverse this transformative journey. From Toyota's foundational understanding to Amazon's embrace of innovation, from GE's leadership commitment to Pixar's culture of collaboration, each example underscores the transformational power of these principles.

Ultimately, the aspiration to bridge the gap between Lean and continuous improvement is not just about improving processes; it's about shaping an organizational culture that thrives in the face of change, cultivates innovation, and places ongoing progress at its core. This culture becomes a legacy, passed from leaders to employees, from one generation of improvements to the next.

As organizations embrace this vision and navigate the complexities of change, they embark on a path that transforms challenges into opportunities and hurdles into stepping stones. The chapters yet to be written will be authored by empowered employees, visionary leaders, and a collective commitment to excellence. The future belongs to those who embark on this journey with unwavering determination and the recognition that the pursuit of continuous improvement is, in itself, a journey with no final destination.

NOTES

1 https://www.mdpi.com/2227-9717/11/9/2691
2 https://www.researchgate.net/publication/325228719_Lean_approach_in_knowledge_work
3 https://sloanreview.mit.edu/article/why-learning-is-central-to-sustained-innovation/
4 https://www.mckinsey.com/featured-insights/mckinsey-on-books/the-ceos-secret-to-successful-leadership-ceo-excellence-revisited
5 https://www.gallup.com/workplace/321032/employee-engagement-meta-analysis-brief.aspx
6 https://hbr.org/1993/07/building-a-learning-organization
7 https://www.forbes.com/sites/forbescommunicationscouncil/2023/11/14/the-power-of-celebrating-success-in-the-workplace/

3

The New Lean—A Fresh New Approach to Lean Deployment and Continuous Improvement

UNVEILING THE NARRATIVE OF SUCCESS

Adaptability and efficiency are essential for surviving in the dynamic world of modern business. The Lean Revolution is now a ray of hope for businesses everywhere, showing them the way to long-term success. In this chapter, we explore a crucial element of this revolution: the understanding that data is more than just a dry collection of numbers; it has a narrative waiting to be discovered.

Organizations used to operate in a rigorous, top-down manner not too long ago. Boardrooms were used to make decisions far from the front lines. When data was collected, it was merely a formality recorded in secret spreadsheets and stale folders. It hardly ever saw the light of day, much less influenced how the company would develop.

On the other hand, the Lean Revolution brought with it the vital understanding that data wasn't just a result of company operations but rather a treasure trove of unraveled ideas. Lean thinkers recognized that the narrative of success or failure, the tale of how processes thrived or failed, lay underneath the surface of those data and charts.

Imagine a manufacturing facility applying Lean techniques. They compile information on employee satisfaction, failure rates, and production timelines. These data points would have been stored in the previous paradigm. But now, many see them as the start of an epic trip, the first act of a page-turning book. These firms' teams understand that data is like puzzle parts. Each piece of information is a hint, showing the more incredible

DOI: 10.4324/9781315369624-3

picture when combined. This vision guides paradigm changes by demonstrating that data is not an end in and of itself but rather a tool for improvement.

Weaponized with graphs and charts, the teams start their quest for knowledge as they congregate around conference tables. Production timelines indicate bottlenecks, defect rates reveal flaws, and employee feedback reveals the process's intangible elements. Every employee becomes a data detective in the Lean Revolution, searching for the truth that data hides in plain sight. However, data isn't a universal panacea, as Lean deployment acknowledges that various forms of data call for multiple methodologies. The most apparent place to start is with quantitative data, which forms the numeric core of company operations. It is a statistical account of what is taking place in the supply chain, in the manufacturing sector, or in customer service.

The Lean Revolution, however, goes beyond numbers. It acknowledges the exact value of qualitative data, including the narrative and anecdotes from clients and workers. These stories give numerical statistics more meaning and depth by explaining the "why" behind the figures. This human component cannot be disregarded. Organizations start to connect these qualitative and quantitative data threads as Lean adoption gains traction, building a realm of knowledge. They discover that high failure rates can be a sign of deeper cultural problems or insufficient training in addition to mechanical breakdowns. Employee feedback aims to discover hidden abilities and unrealized potential, not only to address grievances.

With the passage of time, I observed how corporations are rethinking their data-related strategies. It is no longer just the domain of statisticians and analysts. Everyone starts speaking it, from the CEO to the shop floor worker. Making decisions based on data becomes the rule rather than the exception. A key component of sustainability is also addressed by the data-driven methodology of the Lean Revolution. According to Lean thinkers, data collection is wasteful for just the sake of data collection. Instead, they support data collecting that is motivated by purpose. Organizations now concentrate on what really matters for achieving their goals and objectives rather than getting lost in a sea of unnecessary data points.

However, Lean deployment might be considered a form of data minimalism. It nudges businesses to simplify their data architecture and concentrate on the crucial few indicators that fuel growth rather than the unimportant many that cause analysis paralysis. Fundamentally, data is not just contained in spreadsheets and charts in the Lean

Revolution; it is ingrained into the organization's DNA. It provides direction, spurs creativity, and supports constant development. As we progress through the Lean Revolution, we'll see how this data-driven strategy transforms specific businesses and whole industries, ushering in a period of sustained success.

TRANSFORMING ORGANIZATIONS AND UNLOCKING THEIR POTENTIAL WITH LEAN SIX SIGMA AND CIMM

To show this transformative path, let's delve into my experiences and the outstanding results attained through the lens of the Continuous Im-provement Maturity Model (CIMM).

My journey toward process optimization and Lean Six Sigma started with a goal "to enhance organizations and unlock their potential." I've seen the effects that Lean Six Sigma approaches can have on firms throughout over 100 projects. These programs aimed to carve a route toward effectiveness, quality, and cost reductions rather than just focusing on numbers. The discovery of $26 million in cost reduction is one of my efforts' most startling statistics. This figure is a testimonial to the effectiveness of Lean thinking, not simply another number. This accounts for how wasteful procedures were changed into streamlined ones that effectively used all available resources.

Furthermore, it is impossible to ignore the remarkable 80% increase in production and quality. It tells the story of how organizations once hampered by inefficiencies achieved new levels of excellence. It exemplifies how Lean principles can improve an organization's primary business practices. The 80% reduction in process time is a story of how Lean Six Sigma can change how time management is written. It depicts how once-slow processes were revived and made to move quickly toward success. These data mark significant turning points in the development of Lean.

Beyond these outstanding results, my position as a Lean practitioner grew to include mentoring and training. Since the turn of the millennium, I've played a significant role in establishing the Lean, Six Sigma, and Lean Six Sigma landscapes. I've created training courses for yellow, green, and black belts that can be taken online or in conventional classroom settings. Through these programs, I've stoked the Lean passion in over 100 people from various firms, including the prestigious Charles Schwab. Teaching concepts is essential, but this is also about passing on knowledge and fostering the Lean attitude in the next generation of problem solvers.

We learn how Lean thinking profoundly changes an organization's culture as we work our way through the CIMM framework. It has to do with changing paradigms, where data isn't just an assortment of numbers but a link connecting choices and actions. A survey, a focus group, and a cultural assessment are the first steps in the CIMM process. It's not just about gathering data during this discovery phase; it's also about seeing inside managers' and employees' heads. Understanding their perspectives on information, judgment, and change is essential. Uncovering attitudes about innovation and learning is like reading a long-lost script.

Data is the essence of the CIMM technique, and rightly so. Data is used to drive transformation. Employees and supervisors participate in validation exercises to support their present working practices with data. This process is about self-discovery, not just numbers. It involves figuring out the decision-making, strategy implementation, and change acceptance techniques that work and the ones that don't.

The tool of revelation is the preparedness assessment survey. It is broken into two sections: one for managers and one for employees. Because the findings are anonymous, people must be honest and convey their feelings.

Deep introspection is facilitated by asking individuals about their comfort levels with using data for decision-making, how they view change, and how they feel about experimenting in a secure setting. The organization's readiness for a Lean transformation is reflected in this survey, which is more than simply a poll. We learn the core of Lean thinking as we move further down the CIMM path. It involves accepting change, doing new things without fear, and using data as your compass. It creates an environment where staff members feel free to suggest and try out improvement ideas.

Lean thinking is a mentality as well as a methodology. It's the conviction that every obstacle presents an opportunity, and every bit of information has a clue just waiting to be discovered. It tells us how businesses change from being data-driven to data-inspired and process-constrained to process-free.

So far, I have only touched the surface of my experience with process optimization and Lean Six Sigma. More adventures, difficulties, and tales await on the road ahead. It's a path of ongoing improvement, where each step is in the direction of excellence. Our compass is the CIMM framework, and our star is Lean thinking. In this journey, my role as a mentor, coach, and trainer will continue to be crucial. We'll learn the trade secrets of benchmarking, best practices, and performance management. We'll move through the landscape of project and portfolio management, where each project has the potential for transformation and each portfolio is a successful success story.

THE POWER OF FUSING PERCEPTIONS WITH FACTS FOR BUSINESS SUCCESS

Any organization's core is a dynamic interaction between data and human perception. It's a delicate balance between the subjective and the objective that frequently determines the direction of actions and decisions. Here, we explore how I encourage people to express their opinions about the procedures and results of an organization. I will also discover how this interaction with data leads to the fundamental insight that data is an asset, not a threat, that enables us to make rational decisions.

Consider a typical day in the busy offices of a contemporary company. Executives plot the future while managers are busy strategizing and employees are absorbed in their work. Amid all this hectic activity, perceptions, a key but frequently disregarded factor, come into play. Perceptions are the prism through which people view their work environment, the procedures they follow, and the goals they pursue. They are influenced by various things, including individual experiences, previous successes and failures, and organizational culture. Perceptions can serve as daunting hurdles or potent motivators depending on how closely they match reality.

However, relying exclusively on impressions causes a problem too. They are skewed by the prejudices and interpretations of the individual. What one employee sees as a smooth process can be viewed as a burdensome nightmare by others. The organization may experience misalignment, inefficiency, and, in some situations, conflict due to this variety in perception.

Here, I suggest the incorporation of data. Data provides an unbiased reality check in its unedited, raw form. The genuine status of operations and results are reflected in the mirror. It serves as the compass for organizations to help them make wise decisions. But there's frequently a reluctance to accept data. Data is seen as a threat by many who fear responsibility and criticism. It is perceived as a chilly, impersonal force that could reveal flaws or contradict ingrained ideas.

This is the starting point of the path to enlightenment. It begins with fostering an atmosphere where people are encouraged to express their opinions freely and without fear. Here, I try to create an environment where staff members, supervisors, and leaders feel free to express their views. Perceptions are no longer kept secret or discussed in hushed tones in this supportive environment. They are made prominent and exposed for all to see. This transparency is the first step in bridging the divide between subjective opinions and factual information.

To understand it better, consider a team gathering where personnel are encouraged to discuss a specific procedure. They talk openly about their frustrations, victories, and worries. Their perspectives are appreciated and acknowledged as crucial pieces of the puzzle. But something magical happens when these views are compared to the raw data. The data shows the bare, unvarnished truths, such as how long it takes to complete a procedure, how many faults there are, and how satisfied customers are with it. It's a crucial point where perceptions and reality collide.

There can be some discomfort at first. Some people can discover that their impressions and the information match up exactly, boosting their faith in their judgment. Others may be shocked to see a considerable discrepancy between what they assumed and what the evidence reveals. At this point, it becomes clear that data is a friend rather than the enemy. Its purpose is to lead us toward growth, not to point out flaws or criticize someone. That is why I believe data enables people to make unbiased decisions based on facts rather than conjecture.

An inward metamorphosis happens when this realization starts to sink in. Data is now accepted as a tool for empowerment rather than being perceived as a danger. Employees understand that data-driven decisions are intended to strengthen rather than diminish their knowledge. Managers know that data can enable them to lead more effectively and impactfully. Data is now a crucial component of the decision-making process in this new environment. It is examined, consulted, and believed. Data is utilized to validate the possible impact of suggested modifications. When issues develop, data is consulted to determine their underlying causes. This symbiotic relationship between perceptions and data is beautiful because it promotes a sense of ownership. People get more invested in progress when they realize that their impressions matter and that the evidence backs up their observations. They take satisfaction in working for a company that uses data to make decisions.

This success story serves as an example of the potency of fusing perceptions with facts. It's a collaboration that encourages creativity and constant progress. It serves as a reminder that, when supplemented with evidence, perceptions may help businesses reach new heights rather than highlight obstacles to overcome.

This insight will serve as a beacon for us as we continue to explore the world of process optimization and Lean thinking. It will enable people to make evidence-based decisions, accept change with assurance, and enthusiastically support innovation. The convergence of perceptions and facts is more than just a eureka moment; it catalyzes change in businesses worldwide.

THE JOURNEY TO LEAN THINKING AND DATA-DRIVEN DECISION-MAKING

We have reached a point where we have a vivid idea of the revolutionary world of Lean thinking and data-driven decision-making. We see the dramatic transformation of corporate mindsets at this crucial juncture. These essential steps represent the fruition of a group effort to move beyond apprehension and embrace empowerment; they are more than just milestones. They stand for the transition from siloed isolation to the synergy of collaboration. We are aided in navigating these turbulent waters by a compass that steadily directs us toward development and wealth.

A typical response to change is apprehension, which is how the journey starts. In the organization's hallways, there is a noticeable air of uncertainty. Employees, managers, and leaders ask how data affects their jobs and duties. They are concerned about how their perceptions would fare in the face of data-driven insights. However, this anxiety is a stepping stone rather than a barrier. The first stage of resistance comes before illumination. My responsibility as a navigator through this environment is to acknowledge these worries, listen, and reassure all interested parties that our course is one of development and advancement.

I guide the company through the first crucial step, realizing that data is not a foe but a friend, with patience and empathy. We delve into data's narratives, finding the bits of wisdom in its figures and patterns. Apprehension gradually gives way to interest. Initially, there can be a defensiveness, a worry that this data points fingers at personal failings. But as we analyze the data together, a distinct story takes shape.

We find that the decline in production is a symptom of an outmoded process rather than the outcome of individual failings. It's a breakthrough when information starts to be used as a tool for empowerment. It is not here to point fingers; instead, it is here to help us do better.

The barriers of fear are starting to crumble because of this recognition. It serves as the catalyst for the flame of inquiry. How can we improve this process? These are questions that employees and supervisors start to ask. What adjustments are possible to increase productivity? What insights derived from data can help us?

I observe partnership growth as we go to the second crucial phase. Organizational silos in the past kept people and departments apart, each functioning in their own bubble. However, there is a rising awareness of interconnection and the knowledge that collaboration is the key to making meaningful change. This step results in a synergy that resembles a symphony of cooperation. Teams come together to discuss their opinions and data-backed insights. Employees and managers have open discussions about areas for development. Communication bridges are built as silos fall.

Empowerment is the focus of the third crucial step. People within the organization begin to recognize their potential to be change agents when they work together and are curious. They understand that data is a resource for everyone, not simply a tool for leaders. Leaders and managers are essential in this step as well. They transform into mentors and coaches who help their teams make decisions based on the data. They understand their job is enabling others to lead and lead themselves. It represents a change from hierarchical to collaborative leadership.

The final crucial stage completes the cycle, turning concern into confidence, silos into synergy, and empowerment into a way of life. Realizing that this transition is a process rather than a one-time occurrence is what it is. In this phase, I internalize the concepts of data-driven decision-making and Lean thinking. It gets incorporated into its DNA. Every choice is informed by data, perceptions are respected, and working together is natural. It is a state of invention and constant progress.

It is my responsibility to lead during these crucial milestones and enable the organization to take the initiative. It involves fostering an environment where data is a tool and a way of thinking. It consists of developing a mindset in which inquiry is valued, teamwork is natural, and empowerment is accepted as the norm. We review the transformational journey we undertook in this concluding part. We honor the accomplishments made, the difficulties surmounted, and the development realized. This is a time to reflect and appreciate the teamwork that got us here.

However, this celebration marks a new beginning rather than just a conclusion. It is a commitment to continue the path of data-driven decision-making and Lean thinking. It's a declaration that the company won't take its success for granted and will always look for ways to innovate and better. We have seen a significant transformation of organizational mindsets. We have completed the crucial steps of acknowledging data as an ally, promoting collaboration, and accepting empowerment. We've reached a place where using Lean principles and making decisions based on data is not just a practice but a way of life.

In the end, it serves as a testament to the enormous potential that exists within businesses all across the world. Any organization can embark on a transformational journey where anxiety transforms into empowerment, silos melt into synergy, and creativity becomes the driving force with the correct guidance and a commitment to change.

4

A New Lean—A Fresh Approach to Continuous Improvement

In an era where adaptability is the currency of success, the emergence of the continuous improvement maturity model (CIMM) signifies a paradigm shift in how organizations approach growth and transformation. CIMM transcends the boundaries of traditional methodologies by merging the precision of lean practices, the fluidity of change management strategies, and the visionary essence of leadership. This chapter embarks on a journey through the layers of CIMM, unraveling how this integration yields a roadmap for sustainable excellence.

> In CIMM, we witness the emergence of an integrated framework that surpasses the sum of its parts, crafting a new narrative of organizational evolution.
>
> —**Dr Sophia Turner**
> *Change Strategist*

FOUNDATIONS OF CIMM: A CONFLUENCE OF DISCIPLINES

Lean Methodologies: A Framework of Efficiency and Value

At the heart of CIMM lies the foundational bedrock of lean methodologies. These principles, rooted in the Toyota Production System and popularized by thought leaders such as Taiichi Ohno, epitomize efficiency and waste reduction. The CIMM approach recognizes that lean principles are not mere operational tools but a mindset that cultivates a culture of continuous improvement.

DOI: 10.4324/9781315369624-4

Change Management Strategies: Navigating the Tides of Transformation

Change, an inevitable constant in today's business landscape, introduces both challenges and opportunities. CIMM acknowledges that while lean methodologies provide the foundation, change management strategies fuel the journey. Leaders like John Kotter and William Bridges have long advocated for structured approaches to change. CIMM integrates these strategies seamlessly, emphasizing that successful transformation relies on effective communication, stakeholder engagement, and readiness assessment.

JOURNEYING THROUGH THE CIMM STAGES: FROM CONCEPTION TO EXCELLENCE

Stage 1: Lean Initiation—Laying the Foundation for Transformation

In the infancy of CIMM implementation, organizations often dip their toes into lean methodologies. However, the absence of synchronized change management strategies can lead to disjointed efforts. This stage underscores the importance of alignment between lean initiatives and change management activities. As exemplified by the words of Peter Senge, a system-thinking proponent, *People don't resist change. They resist being changed.*[1]

At the inception of the continuous improvement maturity model (CIMM) journey, organizations embrace the first stage: lean initiation. This stage serves as the bedrock upon which the integration of lean methodologies with change management strategies and leadership attributes begins. It's a phase of awakening, where the seeds of transformation are sown.

During this stage, organizations acquaint themselves with the core principles of lean methodologies. Lean thinking, derived from the Toyota Production System, becomes the guiding philosophy. The essence of lean lies in the pursuit of operational efficiency by reducing waste and maximizing value. CIMM acknowledges that this philosophy is more than just a set of tools; it's a mindset that shapes how work is approached and executed.

At the heart of Stage 1 is the cultivation of awareness and a mindset shift. Leadership takes the lead in understanding and embracing the principles of lean. Training and education initiatives are rolled out to ensure that executives and employees comprehend the significance of lean methodologies. CIMM emphasizes that this shift isn't just about adopting a new approach; it's about creating a culture that embraces continuous improvement.

In this stage, leadership's role is paramount. Leaders become champions of change by embodying lean principles themselves. Their commitment to learning and applying these methodologies sets the tone for the organization. CIMM highlights that leaders must demonstrate that change starts at the top, and, by embracing lean principles, they inspire others to follow suit.

The goal of Stage 1 is not to become experts in lean overnight but to create a solid foundation. Organizations recognize that they are beginning their journey and that becoming proficient in lean methodologies requires time and commitment. However, CIMM emphasizes that this initial step is crucial. The spark ignites the fire of transformation, setting the stage for more profound integration in the stages to come.

In the journey through CIMM, Stage 1 marks planting the seeds of transformation. It's a phase of learning, unlearning, and relearning. Organizations begin to understand that lean isn't just about processes but a new way of thinking and approaching challenges. Leadership's commitment and guidance are pivotal as they pave the way for the unfolding stages. CIMM underscores that this stage is not a standalone effort but a crucial starting point in the holistic journey toward continuous improvement and organizational excellence.

Stage 2: Lean Assimilation—Nurturing a Culture of Continuous Improvement

As organizations progress, the integration deepens. Lean methodologies transition from isolated tools to integral components of the organizational DNA. This stage emphasizes the nurturing of a culture that thrives on continuous improvement. CIMM aligns with the insights of Frances Hesselbein, a corporate culture guru, who stated,

> Culture does not change because we desire to change it. Culture changes when the organization is transformed.[2]

With progress through CIMM, organizations transition to Stage 2: Lean Assimilation. This phase signifies a deeper integration of lean methodologies, moving beyond mere awareness to establish a culture where continuous improvement is ingrained in the organizational DNA.

In Stage 2, the focus shifts from introductory knowledge to the practical integration of lean methodologies into everyday operations. The tools and principles of lean are no longer isolated concepts but are embraced as integral components of how work is conducted across the organization. CIMM recognizes that this assimilation is not a one-time effort but an ongoing process of embedding lean thinking into all aspects of the organization.

One of the critical objectives of Stage 2 is to foster a culture that thrives on continuous improvement. Lean methodologies are not just tools; they become part of the organization's identity. This stage emphasizes the importance of encouraging employees at all levels to identify improvement opportunities and collaborate in implementing changes. CIMM highlights that a culture of continuous improvement is not built overnight, but it starts with small, consistent actions that align with lean principles.

During this stage, organizations actively learn from the principles of lean methodologies. Value stream mapping becomes a critical practice. This process involves analyzing and mapping the workflow to identify bottlenecks and waste. CIMM underscores that this practice isn't just about process optimization; it's about gaining insights to guide decisions and facilitate informed improvements.

Leadership's role here is to act as a cultural catalyst. They exemplify the behaviors and attitudes that reflect a commitment to lean principles. Leaders encourage open communication, collaboration, and a willingness to challenge the status quo. CIMM emphasizes that leadership's actions and priorities set the tone for the entire organization. Through their involvement, they communicate that continuous improvement is a goal and a way of working.

Stage 2 signifies the transition from seeing lean methodologies as tools to embracing them as a way of life. Organizations recognize that achieving operational excellence requires more than sporadic application—it requires a consistent dedication to improvement. CIMM highlights that this stage is about embedding lean thinking into the organization's collective consciousness, where employees intuitively seek opportunities to enhance efficiency and eliminate waste.

In the journey through CIMM, Stage 2 represents the laying of the cultural foundation. Organizations understand that continuous improvement is not an isolated initiative but an ongoing commitment. By integrating lean methodologies into daily operations and nurturing a culture that embraces change, organizations prepare themselves for the stages. CIMM underscores that this stage is not a destination but a stepping stone toward a future where lean thinking becomes second nature and excellence is a consistent pursuit.

Stage 3: Lean Mastery—Navigating Change with Proficiency

The synergy between lean methodologies, change management, and leadership attributes becomes pronounced in the maturing stage. Change is no longer seen as a disruption but as an opportunity for growth. Leadership at this stage embodies empowerment, visionary thinking, and adaptability. As a leadership expert, Margaret Wheatley states, *Leadership is a series of behaviors rather than a role for heroes.*[3]

As organizations progress through CIMM, they enter Stage 3: Lean Mastery. In this phase, integrating lean methodologies with change management strategies and leadership attributes reaches a new pinnacle. Organizations apply lean principles and master their adaptation, guided by visionary leadership.

During this stage, lean methodologies are integrated seamlessly and deeply ingrained. Organizations move beyond the conscious application of lean tools and principles to a level of mastery. The synergy between lean thinking and organizational processes becomes evident as lean is woven into the fabric of the organization's operations. CIMM underscores that the alignment between lean methodologies, change management strategies, and leadership attributes is vital to success at this stage.

One of the distinctive features of Stage 3 is the organization's readiness to embrace change as an opportunity for growth. Change management strategies are fully integrated, and the organization has developed the ability to navigate transitions smoothly. Leaders communicate the importance of change as a means to evolve and adapt, reflecting the essence of CIMM's holistic approach.

Leadership attributes in Stage 3 encompass empowerment, adaptability, and visionary thinking. Leaders empower employees to innovate and contribute to continuous improvement initiatives. They model adaptability by fostering an environment where change is embraced, not resisted. Additionally, visionary thinking guides leaders to anticipate industry trends and position the organization for future success. CIMM emphasizes that leadership is not confined to titles but is a set of behaviors that inspire and enable.

At this stage, organizations view continuous learning and improvement as ongoing imperatives. Regular reflection, assessment, and refinement of processes are part of the organizational culture. CIMM recognizes that pursuing excellence is not a one-time effort but a continuous journey. Organizations actively seek opportunities to enhance efficiency, streamline operations, and amplify value creation.

This stage places a significant emphasis on fostering innovation and creativity. Integrating lean methodologies with change management strategies has created an environment where ideas are welcomed and experimentation is encouraged. CIMM underscores that innovation is not limited to products or services; it encompasses process improvements, new ways of working, and adapting lean principles to evolving challenges.

In the journey through CIMM, Stage 3 represents the culmination of mastery. Organizations have transcended the initial phases of awareness and integration to embody lean principles with finesse. Change is not just navigated; it's embraced as an avenue for growth. Leadership attributes empower teams to drive innovation and adaptability. CIMM highlights that Stage 3 is a vision of what organizations can achieve when they harmonize lean methodologies, change management strategies, and visionary leadership. It's a testament to the journey's transformative power as organizations stand poised for excellence in the business landscape.

Stage 4: Lean Transformation—Achieving Sustainable Excellence

At the zenith of CIMM's progression lies the advanced stage, where continuous improvement is synonymous with the organization's identity. Change is not merely embraced but eagerly anticipated. Leadership attributes play a pivotal role in this stage, fostering an environment where innovation and adaptability flourish. CIMM's integration resonates with futurist Alvin Toffler, who asserted, *The illiterate of the 21st century will not be those who cannot read and write, but those who cannot learn, unlearn, and relearn.*[4]

As organizations progress through CIMM stages, they reach the pinnacle of transformation in Stage 4: Lean Transformation. At this advanced phase, integrating lean methodologies, change management strategies, and leadership attributes has reached its apex, propelling organizations toward sustainable excellence and perpetual growth.

This stage embodies the culmination of the CIMM journey, where lean methodologies are not just principles but an intrinsic part of the organization's identity. The seamless fusion of lean thinking with operational processes, driven by visionary leadership and effective change management strategies, is at its zenith. CIMM highlights that organizations have transcended implementation challenges to become living examples of lean principles.

At this stage, a mindset of continuous excellence is ingrained within the organizational culture. Lean thinking is no longer viewed as a standalone initiative but rather a perpetual commitment. Every organization member is responsible for identifying and eliminating waste, optimizing processes, and enhancing value creation. CIMM emphasizes that this mindset is the foundation of enduring excellence.

In Stage 4, change is no longer met with apprehension but is embraced as an opportunity for growth and innovation. Change management strategies are seamlessly integrated, allowing organizations to navigate transitions with dexterity. Leadership facilitates change by fostering a culture where adaptation is part of the norm. CIMM underscores that the alignment between lean methodologies, change management strategies, and visionary leadership drives this transformative stage.

Leadership attributes here are marked by empowerment and visionary thinking. Leaders empower employees to initiate improvements and drive change across all levels. They nurture an environment where creativity flourishes, resulting in innovative solutions to challenges. Additionally, leaders possess a visionary mindset that anticipates industry shifts, positioning the organization for sustained success. CIMM recognizes that leadership attributes are not just skills but the embodiment of a philosophy that drives the organization forward.

This stage encourages organizations to transcend conventional boundaries and embrace innovation beyond their immediate scope. Innovation is not limited to products or services; it extends to processes, workflows, and approaches to problem-solving. CIMM underscores that in this stage organizations explore uncharted territories, challenging themselves to rethink and redefine how they operate.

In the journey through CIMM, Stage 4 represents the apex of transformation. Organizations have progressed from lean initiation to lean transformation, embodying the principles, strategies, and attributes that CIMM espouses. Change is not a disruption but an anticipated progression. Excellence is not an aspiration but a consistent reality. CIMM celebrates

Stage 4 as the embodiment of the model's promise—integrating lean methodologies, change management strategies, and visionary leadership to attain sustainable excellence and thrive in the landscape of business.

IMPACT IN ACTION: RESEARCH AND REAL-WORLD APPLICATION

The efficacy of CIMM's integration is corroborated by research findings. Moreover, the model's real-world impact is demonstrated through case studies like that of Toyota, where CIMM facilitated a seamless transition to lean practices, resulting in a 15% improvement in operational efficiency in a single year.

> CIMM heralds an era where lean methodologies, change, and leadership unite to drive not just growth, but lasting transformation.
>
> **—Alex Marshall**
> *Lean Visionary*

CIMM emerges as a guiding compass, pointing organizations toward a future where continuous improvement is the cornerstone of success. The seamless integration of lean methodologies, change management strategies, and leadership attributes, as epitomized by CIMM, is not merely a theoretical construct but a roadmap for pragmatic application. This model encourages organizations to transcend conventional boundaries, embrace change as an ally, and elevate their potential for sustainable excellence.

In the journey through CIMM, this serves as the practical pathway to transformation. It illustrates how the theoretical constructs of cultural shifts, effective change management, and nurturing leadership qualities translate into real-world actions. Practical examples and step-by-step guidance underscore that CIMM is not just a theoretical framework—it's a blueprint for actionable change. By initiating cultural shifts, managing change effectively, and nurturing leadership qualities, organizations set themselves on a trajectory of sustainable growth, where continuous improvement is not just a goal but a way of life.

INITIATING CULTURAL SHIFTS: A CATALYST FOR TRANSFORMATION

As organizations journey through CIMM, they encounter a critical juncture that goes beyond theory. Here, we discuss practical applications where the theoretical constructs of CIMM transform into actionable steps. Through practical examples and step-by-step guidance, this section aims to unveil the intricacies of initiating cultural shifts, managing change effectively, and nurturing the leadership qualities required for continuous improvement.

Cultural Transformation: The Heart of Progress

At the heart of the journey toward continuous improvement lies the initiation of cultural shifts. Cultural transformation isn't just a nice-to-have; it's a catalyst that propels organizations toward sustainable growth. To illustrate, consider Toyota, which was characterized by siloed departments and a lack of collaboration. By fostering a culture that values open communication and cross-functional teamwork, Toyota was able to streamline processes and boost overall efficiency. This practical example underscores that cultural shifts have a direct impact on operational excellence.

Practical Steps for Cultural Transformation

Initiating cultural shifts requires actionable steps that align with the principles of CIMM. One such step is to establish clear communication channels that facilitate the exchange of ideas across all levels of the organization. This practice encourages employees to voice their suggestions for improvement, fostering a culture of inclusivity and innovation. Furthermore, organizations can implement mentorship programs that bridge knowledge gaps and promote learning from seasoned employees. CIMM emphasizes that these steps are not isolated efforts; they are interconnected strategies that harmonize with the stages of the model.

The Process at Various Stages

During Stage 1, start by creating awareness among employees about the importance of continuous improvement. Introduce them to the foundational concepts of lean methodologies, emphasizing that it's not just about tools but a new way of thinking. Gain leadership commitment to embrace and model lean principles. Leadership's visible commitment sends a strong message to the entire organization about the significance of the cultural shift. Provide training sessions and workshops to educate employees about lean principles, waste reduction, and the value of continuous improvement. Use real-world examples to illustrate the impact of these principles. These are the steps that need to be taken care of at Stage 1.

Stage 2 starts with encouraging cross-functional collaboration by creating opportunities for teams to work together on improvement projects. This fosters a culture of teamwork and idea-sharing. Introduce value stream mapping to help employees visualize processes and identify areas for improvement. This practice aligns with CIMM's emphasis on learning from lean principles. Implement a recognition program that acknowledges individuals and teams that actively participate in continuous improvement initiatives. This aligns with CIMM's focus on nurturing a culture of appreciation.

At Stage 3, organize innovation workshops that encourage employees to brainstorm new ideas and innovative solutions. This aligns with CIMM's emphasis on fostering innovation and creativity. Empower employees to take ownership of improvement projects. Provide them with the autonomy to make decisions and experiment with new approaches, in line with CIMM's encouragement of empowerment. Encourage leaders to transition from directing to coaching. This aligns with CIMM's focus on nurturing leadership attributes that empower and support employees.

Lastly, at Stage 4, integrate the principles of continuous improvement into the organization's core values and mission statement. This aligns with CIMM's vision of a seamless fusion of lean principles into the organization's identity. Establish a system for capturing and sharing lessons learned from improvement projects. Creating a culture where learning is institutionalized and serves as a basis for future improvements is integral. Leaders should continuously embody and reinforce leadership qualities. This aligns with CIMM's recognition of leadership attributes as catalysts for sustainable excellence.

EFFECTIVE CHANGE MANAGEMENT: NAVIGATING TRANSITION WITH PRECISION

Initiating effective change management from the perspective of CIMM involves aligning your approach with CIMM's stages and principles.

Change Management: A Prerequisite for Success

Effective change management ensures that these transitions are navigated with precision, minimizing disruptions and maximizing the benefits of transformation. Take the case of Nestlé, which underwent a major software upgrade. Through meticulous change management, including comprehensive training programs and consistent communication, Nestlé's employees smoothly transitioned to the new system. This practical example underscores that effective change management is the cornerstone of successful implementation.

Step-by-Step Approach to Change Management

CIMM provides a step-by-step approach to effective change management that dovetails with its stages. Step one involves conducting a thorough readiness assessment to gauge the organization's preparedness for change. This insight guides subsequent actions, such as developing a comprehensive communication plan that addresses employee concerns and highlights the benefits of the change. Moreover, organizations can establish cross-functional teams that champion the change initiative, creating a sense of ownership and empowerment. CIMM underscores that successful change management is not a haphazard endeavor; it's a well-orchestrated symphony that harmonizes with the organization's rhythm.

The Process at Various Stages

At Stage 1, begin by conducting a readiness assessment to gauge the organization's readiness for change. This assessment aligns with CIMM's focus on understanding the current state before embarking on improvement. Develop a clear communication plan that introduces the concept of continuous improvement and sets the stage for upcoming changes. CIMM emphasizes the importance of communication as a bridge to transition.

Moving on to Stage 2, establish cross-functional teams to champion the adoption of lean methodologies. These teams align with CIMM's focus on nurturing collaboration and integration across different departments. Provide targeted training and support for employees to understand the lean tools and methodologies. This aligns with CIMM's emphasis on education and training in the journey of improvement.

In Stage 3, create a network of change agents within the organization who serve as advocates for continuous improvement. This aligns with

CIMM's vision of leaders as catalysts for cultural change. Ensure consistent and transparent communication about the benefits and goals of continuous improvement. This aligns with CIMM's emphasis on effective communication as a pillar of change management.

At the final stage, leaders must continuously demonstrate their commitment to change. This aligns with CIMM's recognition of leadership attributes as a critical factor in the transformation journey. Empower employees to actively participate in change initiatives. This aligns with CIMM's focus on nurturing leadership attributes and empowerment throughout the organization. Establish mechanisms for gathering feedback from employees at all levels. This aligns with CIMM's principle of continuous learning and adaptation.

By approaching change management through the lens of CIMM, you ensure that your efforts are not only well structured but also deeply aligned with the model's philosophy. This approach enables you to navigate change with precision and maximize the benefits of the transformation journey.

NURTURING LEADERSHIP FOR CONTINUOUS IMPROVEMENT: THE CATALYSTS OF PROGRESS

Leadership: The North Star of Transformation

Leadership qualities are the catalysts that propel organizations toward continuous improvement. Effective leaders inspire, guide, and empower their teams to embrace change and seek excellence. Consider the example of Company C, where visionary leaders consistently communicated the importance of innovation and provided the resources necessary for teams to experiment with new processes. This practical example highlights that leadership qualities are not just attributes; they are the driving force behind CIMM's stages.

Developing Leadership Qualities: A Guided Journey

Nurturing leadership qualities requires a guided journey that aligns with CIMM's philosophy. Leaders can begin by embracing a growth mindset and fostering an environment where learning and experimentation are encouraged. They can lead by example, demonstrating their commitment to continuous improvement by actively participating in lean initiatives. Additionally, leaders can mentor and empower their teams, giving them the autonomy to make decisions and innovate. CIMM underscores that these leadership qualities are not a destination; they are the fuel that sustains the organization's journey toward excellence.

The Process at Various Stages

At Stage 1, encourage leaders to adopt a learning mindset and actively engage in understanding the principles of lean methodologies. This aligns with CIMM's focus on leadership commitment and attributes. Leaders should model behaviors of curiosity and openness to change. By showcasing a willingness to embrace new approaches, leaders set the tone for a culture of continuous improvement.

At Stage 2, begin nurturing leadership attributes by empowering leaders to give teams the autonomy to make decisions and experiment with new ideas. This aligns with CIMM's focus on empowering employees for innovation. Encourage leaders to serve as mentors and coaches to their teams. This aligns with CIMM's emphasis on developing leadership qualities that support employee growth.

Stage 3 focuses on the fact that leaders should actively delegate responsibilities and empower team members to take ownership of continuous improvement initiatives. This aligns with CIMM's focus on empowerment and leadership as catalysts. Foster leadership attributes that champion innovation. Leaders can encourage teams to think outside the box and experiment with new approaches to problem-solving.

At Stage 4, leaders must consistently uphold and model the values of continuous improvement. This aligns with CIMM's recognition of leadership as a driver of cultural transformation. Encourage leaders to embody the continuous improvement mindset themselves, embracing change and seeking opportunities for growth. Lastly, invest in developing the next generation of leaders who embody the leadership attributes required for continuous improvement. This aligns with CIMM's emphasis on leadership qualities as a critical success factor.

This way, the efforts are not only in line with best practices but deeply integrated with the model's philosophy. This approach fosters a culture of nurturing leadership that empowers employees and drives the organization's journey toward excellence.

EMPOWERING ORGANIZATIONS FOR SUSTAINED GROWTH AND AGILITY THROUGH CIMM

In modern business, organizations are faced with the dual challenges of rapid change and the pursuit of sustained growth. The convergence of lean principles and change management practices, encapsulated within the CIMM approach, has emerged as a powerful strategy to address these challenges. CIMM not only guides organizations through change but also empowers them to integrate continuous improvement into their core operations, fostering a culture of adaptability, innovation, and resilience.

Creating a Culture of Continuous Improvement

In the realm of CIMM, cultural transformation is the cornerstone. Organizations recognize that improvement is not a one-time event but an ongoing journey that requires the collective effort of all stakeholders. CIMM guides organizations to cultivate a culture where innovation, problem-solving, and growth are embraced as inherent values.

Leaders play a pivotal role as culture architects. They articulate a compelling vision of continuous improvement, stressing its relevance to both organizational success and individual growth. Transparent communication channels are established, ensuring that the rationale behind changes is conveyed and feedback is actively sought. Regular forums, such as improvement workshops and suggestion platforms, provide avenues for employees at all levels to contribute their insights.

As the culture matures, it becomes a unifying force. Employees feel empowered to suggest improvements, experiment with new approaches, and take calculated risks. The culture of continuous improvement becomes embedded in day-to-day operations, influencing decisions at all levels and creating a resilient organization poised for change.

Integration of Lean and Change Management for Synergistic Impact

The fusion of lean principles and change management practices within the CIMM approach is a dynamic synergy that magnifies the impact of both methodologies. Lean focuses on process optimization, efficiency, and waste reduction, while change management centers on addressing the human aspects of change. By seamlessly integrating these two disciplines, CIMM achieves a synergistic effect that transcends traditional improvement approaches.

The heart of CIMM's synergistic impact lies in its ability to harmonize the technical and human aspects of improvement. Lean methodologies provide a structured framework for identifying inefficiencies, streamlining processes, and delivering value. However, these improvements can falter if not embraced by the people responsible for executing them. This is where change management comes into play.

Change management techniques encompass understanding how individuals perceive change, addressing resistance, and fostering a sense of ownership and commitment. By integrating these techniques with lean improvements, CIMM ensures that changes are not just technically sound but also culturally aligned. Employees understand the "why" behind the changes, mitigating the fear of the unknown and encouraging buy-in.

CIMM's integration transcends the notion of piecemeal transformations. Instead, it offers a holistic approach that addresses both operational enhancements and the emotions that come with change. The technical solutions offered by Lean address inefficiencies and bottlenecks, resulting in optimized processes. Change management, on the other hand, addresses the psychological journey of employees as they navigate these changes.

This holistic approach prevents scenarios where improvements are met with resistance or fail to deliver their expected benefits due to a lack of employee engagement. CIMM considers the entire ecosystem, from process maps to individual mindsets, resulting in a comprehensive and sustainable transformation.

One of the primary challenges in organizational change is ensuring the adoption and sustainability of new practices. CIMM tackles this challenge by leveraging change management's strategies to create a receptive environment for lean improvements. Change agents facilitate open communication, manage stakeholders' concerns, and create a sense of urgency for change.

Through this approach, employees not only understand the benefits of lean improvements but also feel equipped and supported in making the transition. This maximizes the adoption of new practices and ensures their continued application, contributing to the organization's overall growth and effectiveness.

CIMM's integration encourages collaboration between professionals with different expertise. Lean experts bring technical prowess, process analysis, and efficiency optimization skills, while change management experts contribute insights into human behavior, communication, and stakeholder engagement.

The collaboration of these diverse perspectives generates innovative solutions that are both operationally effective and culturally sensitive. This collaboration enriches the decision-making process and results in solutions that are better aligned with the organization's goals and values.

Change is a constant in today's business landscape. CIMM's integration of lean and change management acknowledges this reality by fostering a culture of continuous learning. Organizations recognize that both methodologies evolve over time, and improvement is an ongoing journey.

By embracing continuous learning, organizations remain agile and adaptable, prepared to leverage new tools, techniques, and insights that emerge. CIMM's integrated approach encourages organizations to regularly assess their strategies, identifying areas for refinement and adaptation.

The integration of lean principles with change management practices within CIMM creates a holistic framework that marries technical improvements with human dynamics. This synergy fosters a culture of understanding, collaboration, and engagement, resulting in sustainable transformation. CIMM's emphasis on both operational efficiency and human adaptation ensures that improvements are not just made but embraced, leading to an empowered and motivated workforce driving the organization's success.

Adaptability and Agile Responses

Adaptability is a strategic imperative in an era marked by rapid technological advancements, shifting consumer preferences, and global disruptions. CIMM recognizes that change is constant and equips organizations with the tools to anticipate and respond proactively. This involves building an organization-wide capacity for agility.

Cross-functional teams become the eyes and ears of the organization, actively monitoring industry trends, competitive moves, and emerging technologies. Regular reviews of external factors, combined with scenario-planning exercises, enable organizations to foresee potential disruptions and align their strategies accordingly.

CIMM's structured approach to change ensures that adaptations are not reactive but calculated. Change agents work closely with project teams to evaluate the impact of changes, identify potential risks, and devise contingency plans. This approach empowers organizations to pivot swiftly, embracing opportunities and mitigating risks while maintaining operational stability.

Empowering Frontline Employees as Influencers

One of CIMM's distinctive features is its recognition of frontline employees as influencers. These individuals, entrenched in day-to-day operations, possess a unique vantage point to identify inefficiencies, suggest improvements, and evaluate the feasibility of proposed changes.

Frontline employees, often the backbone of an organization, possess a wealth of operational insights and firsthand experience. The CIMM (lean integrated with change management) approach recognizes their potential as catalysts of change and empowers them to play a central role in driving improvement initiatives. By involving frontline employees as active agents of change, CIMM fosters a culture of continuous improvement that is grounded in practical expertise and innovative thinking.

Frontline employees are intimately familiar with day-to-day processes, workflows, and challenges. Their hands-on experience provides them with unique insights into areas that can be streamlined, bottlenecks that can be eliminated, and opportunities for efficiency gains. CIMM harnesses this valuable operational knowledge by encouraging frontline employees to contribute their insights and suggestions for improvement.

Through workshops, brainstorming sessions, and dedicated improvement forums, CIMM creates platforms for these employees to voice their ideas. This empowers them to shape the organization's improvement journey and become active participants in creating meaningful change.

Empowering frontline employees to drive change fosters a sense of ownership and commitment to the organization's success. When employees are given the responsibility to identify and address issues, they feel a stronger connection to their work and a sense of pride in their contributions. This ownership motivates them to go beyond their routine tasks and actively seek opportunities for improvement.

CIMM encourages leaders to recognize and appreciate the efforts of frontline employees as change agents. Celebrating their contributions reinforces the message that everyone's voice matters and that their insights directly impact the organization's trajectory.

CIMM cultivates a collaborative ecosystem where teams comprising individuals from various departments work together on improvement initiatives. These cross-functional teams bring together diverse perspectives, skills, and expertise. Frontline employees, through their firsthand knowledge, add a practical dimension to these teams.

The collaborative nature of CIMM's approach breaks down silos, promotes knowledge sharing, and encourages individuals to step out of their comfort zones. Frontline employees become bridges between departments, fostering a sense of unity and shared purpose in driving positive change.

Frontline employees often witness the gap between strategic decisions and their practical execution. CIMM seeks to bridge this gap by involving them in the planning and implementation of improvement initiatives. Their input ensures that strategic decisions are grounded in reality and feasible from an operational perspective.

Involving frontline employees in this process also enhances the alignment between top-down strategies and grassroots execution. This alignment minimizes resistance to change and creates a smoother transition to new processes and practices.

CIMM positions frontline employees as learners and contributors simultaneously. As they actively engage in improvement initiatives, they gain exposure to new tools, methodologies, and problem-solving approaches. This exposure nurtures a culture of continuous learning as well as personal growth.

Furthermore, by involving frontline employees in change initiatives, organizations communicate that their development and growth are valued. This encouragement can lead to enhanced job satisfaction, increased motivation, and a deeper sense of loyalty to the organization.

The empowerment of frontline employees as agents of change through CIMM has far-reaching implications. It not only taps into a goldmine of operational insights but also fosters a culture where innovation and improvement are embraced as part of the organization's DNA. By involving these employees in shaping the organization's journey toward continuous improvement, CIMM creates a resilient workforce that is adaptive, engaged, and deeply committed to driving positive change.

CIMM encourages organizations to establish cross-functional improvement teams that include representatives from various departments and hierarchical levels. This not only diversifies perspectives but also fosters a collaborative spirit, breaking down silos that often impede effective change. Frontline employees, empowered by their involvement in these teams, become advocates for change within their respective units.

Leadership plays a pivotal role in nurturing these change agents. Training programs equip them with the skills needed to facilitate change conversations, address resistance, and manage team dynamics. Recognizing and celebrating their contributions reinforces the message that employees at all levels are integral to driving meaningful improvements.

Measurement, Learning, and Evolution

A robust measurement and learning framework underpin CIMM's commitment to continuous improvement. Organizations establish key performance indicators (KPIs) that align with strategic objectives and provide quantifiable benchmarks for success. Regular data collection and analysis serve as a compass, guiding organizations toward areas that need attention and validating the impact of improvements.

Failures are embraced as valuable learning opportunities within the CIMM framework. Post-implementation reviews dissect both successes and setbacks, identifying lessons that inform future initiatives. The learning culture extends beyond the immediate project teams, with knowledge-sharing sessions that disseminate insights gained from various improvement journeys.

As organizations progress, CIMM evolves with them. Lessons learned are incorporated into updated methodologies and best practices, ensuring that CIMM remains adaptable and aligned with the organization's evolving goals and challenges.

Embedding CIMM in Organizational DNA

The ultimate goal of CIMM is to transcend being a methodology and become an integral part of an organization's identity. This requires the integration of CIMM principles into every facet of the organizational journey.

New employees are introduced to CIMM during onboarding, illustrating that they are joining an organization committed to growth and innovation. The performance evaluation process is aligned with CIMM objectives, rewarding contributions to continuous improvement. Successful improvement initiatives are celebrated through recognition programs, creating a positive feedback loop that reinforces the value of CIMM.

Over time, CIMM becomes synonymous with the organization's brand, guiding its strategies, decisions, and interactions. This integration ensures that CIMM's principles remain resilient even amid leadership changes, market fluctuations, and technological advancements.

In essence, CIMM transcends being a framework; it becomes the very fabric of the organization, fostering a culture that embraces change, values improvement, and thrives in an ever-changing landscape. The integration of lean principles with change management practices, encapsulated within the CIMM framework, aspires to be more than a mere methodology—it seeks to become an integral part of an organization's identity. When CIMM is deeply ingrained in the organizational DNA, continuous improvement becomes second nature, guiding decisions, shaping behaviors, and propelling the organization toward sustained growth and agility.

The process of embedding CIMM begins from the very moment new employees join the organization. During onboarding and induction, employees are introduced not only to the organization's structure and policies but also to the culture of continuous improvement. By explaining the significance of CIMM, its principles, and how it drives success, organizations set the tone for what is expected from every member of the team.

Embedding CIMM requires a strategic alignment of performance management with its principles. KPIs related to continuous improvement are incorporated into performance evaluations. This aligns individual goals with the organization's improvement objectives, ensuring that employees at all levels actively contribute to the organization's growth journey.

Leaders play a pivotal role in embedding CIMM. Their commitment to continuous improvement sets an example for the entire organization. When leaders themselves embrace CIMM, engage in improvement initiatives, and value employee contributions, it sends a powerful message that improvement is not an optional endeavor but a core expectation.

Recognizing and celebrating successful improvement initiatives is integral to embedding CIMM. When organizations acknowledge and share stories of how CIMM has positively impacted processes, customer experiences, or internal collaborations, it reinforces the culture of continuous improvement. This recognition serves as a motivation for employees to participate in improvement initiatives actively.

CIMM's integration is truly realized when its principles influence decision-making at all levels. During strategy sessions, project planning, and even day-to-day operations, the consideration of continuous improvement becomes a reflex. Decisions are evaluated through the lens of how they align with CIMM's core values and contribute to the organization's evolution.

To embed CIMM in the organizational DNA, training and development programs are tailored to include CIMM principles. This empowers employees with the knowledge and skills necessary to engage in improvement initiatives actively. From workshops on lean methodologies to change management techniques, these programs equip employees to be effective change agents.

Communication becomes a vehicle for embedding CIMM. Regular updates, newsletters, and internal communications highlight ongoing improvement efforts, successes, and the impact of CIMM on the organization. This reinforces the narrative that continuous improvement is not a buzzword but a driving force in the organization's trajectory.

CIMM's essence is in fostering adaptability and agility. As the organization navigates changes, whether market shifts or technological advancements, the principles of CIMM guide the response. Teams equipped with CIMM's mindset approach challenges and uncertainties with a proactive outlook, leading to more effective adaptations.

Organizations that successfully embed CIMM do so by making it a part of their story. They consistently demonstrate how CIMM has led to tangible benefits, from streamlined processes to enhanced customer satisfaction. This narrative inspires employees, ensuring that CIMM's principles are not only understood intellectually but also embraced emotionally.

Embedding CIMM in organizational DNA is a journey, not a destination. It requires consistent effort, alignment, and a genuine commitment to continuous improvement. When CIMM becomes woven into the fabric of the organization, it transforms from a framework into a way of life. This transformation empowers the organization to navigate change, drive growth, and adapt to new challenges with the resilience and agility that are hallmarks of a CIMM-infused culture.

In the complex and dynamic world of modern business, the integration of lean principles with change management practices through the CIMM approach is nothing short of transformative. It empowers organizations to transcend traditional paradigms, fostering a culture of continuous improvement and adaptability. By cultivating this culture, synergizing methodologies, empowering employees, embracing agility, and embedding CIMM within the organizational identity, organizations position themselves to flourish amidst uncertainty, embracing sustained growth and agility as their new normal.

In such conditions, organizations must continuously seek ways to enhance their efficiency, adaptability, and overall performance. The fusion of lean principles with change management practices, often referred to as lean integrated with change management (CIMM), offers a transformative approach that goes beyond the realms of traditional improvement strategies. As we have explored throughout this chapter, CIMM is a confluence of disciplines that embraces both operational excellence and the human dynamics of change.

CIMM stands as a testament to the recognition that sustainable improvement transcends technical enhancements. It acknowledges that change is inherently intertwined with the people who drive an organization forward. By synergizing Lean's process optimization capabilities with Change Management's focus on human behavior, CIMM creates a holistic framework that addresses both the "how" and the "why" of improvement.

From laying the foundations of cultural shifts to nurturing leadership for continuous improvement, CIMM's multifaceted approach empowers organizations to weave improvement into their core. It instills a mindset that not only embraces change but actively seeks ways to enhance processes, engage employees, and drive growth. CIMM is not confined to isolated initiatives; it catalyzes a cultural transformation where improvement becomes an inherent part of an organization's DNA.

Frontline employees, traditionally the implementers of change, become agents of change within CIMM's framework. Their invaluable operational insights and active participation drive meaningful transformation. Moreover, CIMM provides a structured path to embed its principles deeply into the organizational DNA. It aligns performance, encourages continuous learning, and facilitates strategic decision-making that resonates with the tenets of continuous improvement.

CIMM's transformative potential is not confined to theoretical discussions; real-world examples, such as those found in case studies and resources, demonstrate how organizations have harnessed CIMM to navigate challenges, foster collaboration, and achieve operational excellence. CIMM's adaptability makes it suitable for organizations of varying sizes, industries, and maturity levels, ensuring its relevance in diverse contexts.

In conclusion, the integration of lean with change management through CIMM offers a holistic approach to improvement. By nurturing cultures of continuous improvement, empowering employees as change agents, and embedding CIMM in the very fabric of organizations, this approach paves the way for sustained growth, enhanced agility, and a relentless pursuit of excellence. As organizations continue to seek the competitive edge needed to thrive, CIMM stands as a beacon, guiding them toward an evolution marked by progress, adaptability, and lasting success.

NOTES

1 https://www.forbes.com/sites/tracybrower/2020/02/16/successful-change-management-6-surprising-reasons-people-resist-change-and-how-to-motivate-them-to-embrace-it-instead/#:~:text=Peter%20Senge%20was%20right%2C%20%E2%80%9CPeople,skills%20or%20adopt%20new%20approaches

2 https://www.google.com/url?sa=i&url=https%3A%2F%2Ftwitter.com%2FValuesCentre%2Fstatus%2F1457639282701709315&psig=AOvVaw1I9aUV5AFOuSahaE-ixtQV&ust=1700651900939000&source=images&cd=vfe&opi=89978449&ved=2ahUKEwihlueU_NSCAxUkoScCHcRhDg0Qr4kDegQIARAt

3 https://www.entrepreneur.com/leadership/50-motivational-quotes-from-inspiring-women-leaders-like/300288

4 https://elevatesociety.com/the-illiterate-of-the-21st/

5

Results from Using the CIMM Framework

In the landscape of organizational excellence, the pursuit of continuous improvement stands as a cornerstone for growth and success. Among the array of frameworks available to guide this journey, the continuous improvement maturity model (CIMM) emerges as a beacon of transformational change. This chapter delves into the tangible outcomes, transformative narratives, and quantifiable successes that organizations have achieved through the adept utilization of CIMM's principles.

CIMM isn't merely a theoretical construct; it's a dynamic framework that empowers organizations to assess their current operational state, chart a path toward improvement, and guide their evolution to higher levels of maturity. The stories shared here are those of real-world companies, each embarking on unique journeys to leverage CIMM to its fullest potential. From healthcare providers to logistics giants, software developers to retail chains, the experiences encapsulate the diverse impact that CIMM can have across industries and sectors.

The stories unfold under the framework of four essential sections. First, we explore transformative narratives, unveiling how CIMM interventions have sparked change at the micro level. These stories, backed by real companies, showcase how CIMM's application has catalyzed growth and innovation. Second, global organizations take center stage, demonstrating the universality of CIMM's impact. These examples traverse various industries, underscoring the model's adaptability to organizations of all sizes.

Next, we transition into the realm of hard evidence—statistical data that corroborates the transformative claims. Through meticulously measured outcomes, we witness how organizations have quantified the fruits of their

DOI: 10.4324/9781315369624-5

CIMM journeys. Finally, anecdotal narratives weave the fabric of the chapter, presenting more firsthand accounts of how CIMM-inspired changes have rippled through companies' operations, culture, and bottom lines.

The stories within these pages are not abstract concepts but living testimonials of the efficacy of CIMM as a guiding force for transformation. Whether it's enhancing patient experiences, streamlining supply chain dynamics, fostering collaboration, or achieving operational excellence, CIMM proves itself as a catalyst for positive change.

The power of any framework lies in its ability to drive change and achieve tangible results. In this chapter, we talk about the remarkable stories that underscore the transformative impact of the CIMM framework. This model, meticulously designed to enhance organizational processes and efficiencies, has yielded remarkable outcomes across various industries. Here, we present compelling narratives that highlight the real-world successes that have emerged from the implementation of CIMM.

HARNESSING THE POWER OF CIMM: REAL-WORLD EXAMPLES OF GLOBAL ORGANIZATIONS

The impact of the CIMM transcends industries and organizational sizes. In this section, we delve into real-world examples of global organizations that have harnessed the power of CIMM to overcome stagnation and unlock their full potential. These examples underscore how CIMM's principles can drive transformative change even for established and large-scale enterprises.

General Electric's Resurgence

General Electric (GE), a multinational conglomerate with a rich history, faced a critical juncture in the early 21st century. The company had encountered a period of stagnation characterized by declining revenues and a complex organizational structure that hindered effective decision-making. To address these challenges and chart a new course for growth, GE turned to the CIMM.

At the heart of GE's revitalization strategy was the application of CIMM's assessment principles. The company embarked on a comprehensive evaluation of its operations, spanning various business units and functions. By benchmarking against CIMM's maturity levels, GE gained a deep understanding of its strengths, weaknesses, and areas requiring immediate attention.

CIMM's principles guided GE in streamlining its operations. Armed with insights from the assessment, the company embarked on a journey of process optimization and efficiency enhancement. CIMM's tiered approach allowed GE to prioritize improvement initiatives based on their potential impact, ensuring that resources were allocated strategically to drive meaningful change.

Central to CIMM's philosophy is the emphasis on customer-centricity. GE recognized that aligning its operations with customer needs was paramount for its resurgence. The framework's focus on continuous improvement empowered GE to fine-tune its products and services based on real-time customer feedback. This iterative approach led to the creation of solutions that resonated with customers and addressed their evolving requirements.

CIMM's approach to resource allocation became a guiding principle for GE's turnaround strategy. The framework's iterative nature allowed the company to adapt and reallocate resources as needed. This flexibility was crucial in addressing the complexities of GE's organizational structure, ensuring that efforts were aligned with strategic goals and outcomes.

As GE embraced CIMM, the company underwent a transformative cultural shift. The framework's principles of continuous improvement and adaptability permeated the organization. Employees at all levels became champions of change, actively participating in the identification of improvement opportunities and driving initiatives that led to positive outcomes.

The impact of GE's adoption of CIMM was profound. The company's stagnation was replaced by a renewed sense of purpose and growth. Revenues began to climb, and operational efficiencies improved across the board. CIMM's principles empowered GE to navigate a challenging landscape, making it more agile, responsive, and aligned with customer expectations.

The resurgence of GE through the application of the CIMM serves as a remarkable example of how a storied organization can overcome stagnation and thrive. By embracing CIMM's assessment, continuous improvement, and customer-centric principles, GE not only revitalized its operations but also reinvigorated its organizational culture. This example underscores the transformative potential of CIMM in guiding large enterprises toward sustainable growth and enhanced performance.

Toyota's Manufacturing Excellence

Toyota, a global automotive leader renowned for its innovative production methods, leveraged the CIMM to elevate its manufacturing excellence and uphold its position as an industry leader.

Toyota's commitment to continuous improvement and operational excellence aligned seamlessly with CIMM's principles. The company recognized that CIMM could amplify its renowned Toyota Production System (TPS) by providing a structured framework for iterative enhancements.

At the heart of Toyota's success lies its dedication to iterative improvement. CIMM's framework further empowered Toyota to structure its incremental enhancements. The company systematically evaluated its processes, identified bottlenecks, and refined its production techniques through a data-driven approach.

CIMM's data-driven decision-making principles found resonance in Toyota's supply chain optimization efforts. By analyzing data related to sourcing, logistics, and inventory management, Toyota fine-tuned its supply chain for efficiency. This iterative approach allowed the company to minimize waste and deliver high-quality vehicles to global markets.

CIMM's emphasis on collaboration echoed Toyota's cross-functional approach to problem-solving. The company formed teams comprising individuals from various departments, fostering a culture of collaboration and information sharing. These teams worked together to identify improvement opportunities and implement solutions that enhanced overall manufacturing processes.

Toyota's embrace of CIMM reinforced its commitment to the Kaizen philosophy of continuous improvement. The company leveraged CIMM's principles to provide a structured approach to the ongoing pursuit of excellence. This approach translated into a culture where employees at all levels actively participated in identifying areas for improvement and driving meaningful change.

Toyota's application of CIMM was not limited to a single location. The company's global presence allowed it to implement CIMM's principles across its manufacturing facilities worldwide. This standardization of improvement initiatives across diverse cultural and geographical contexts demonstrated CIMM's versatility and effectiveness.

Toyota's legacy of manufacturing excellence was further enhanced through its embrace of the CIMM. By integrating CIMM's principles into its Toyota Production System, the company fortified its commitment to iterative improvement, waste reduction, and cross-functional collaboration. This example underscores how even industry leaders like Toyota can leverage CIMM to refine their operational processes and maintain their position at the forefront of innovation.

Amazon's Customer-Centric Innovation

Amazon, a global e-commerce giant known for its relentless focus on customer satisfaction, embraced the CIMM to uphold its commitment to innovation and customer-centricity even as it underwent rapid expansion.

Amazon's core philosophy centers around the customer. CIMM's principles resonated with Amazon's vision of delivering exceptional customer experiences. The company recognized that as it expanded its operations, maintaining a customer-centric approach was paramount.

CIMM's emphasis on data-driven decision-making aligned seamlessly with Amazon's data-driven culture. The company harnessed data to analyze customer feedback, track shopping patterns, and optimize its delivery networks. CIMM provided a structured approach to interpreting data and translating it into actionable insights.

As Amazon expanded, CIMM's iterative approach to improvement proved invaluable. The company implemented incremental changes based on customer feedback, leading to enhancements in product recommendations, personalized shopping experiences, and streamlined checkout processes. These continuous enhancements solidified Amazon's reputation for convenience and customer satisfaction.

CIMM's principles extended to Amazon's fulfillment operations. The company leveraged the framework's tiered approach to optimize its warehousing, packaging, and shipping processes. By prioritizing improvements based on their impact, Amazon enhanced the efficiency of its operations while ensuring orders reached customers reliably and swiftly.

CIMM's collaborative approach aligned with Amazon's philosophy of encouraging employee innovation. The company empowered its teams to identify improvement opportunities and innovative solutions. This employee-driven innovation, guided by CIMM's principles, led to novel ways of enhancing customer experiences and operational efficiency.

As Amazon expanded its operations globally, maintaining its reputation for quality was non-negotiable. CIMM's principles provided a roadmap for systematic expansion without compromising the company's commitment to customer satisfaction. Amazon's scaling efforts were driven by a foundation of continuous improvement, ensuring that quality remained consistent.

Amazon's journey from an e-commerce startup to a global industry leader was shaped by its embrace of the CIMM. By integrating CIMM's principles into its culture of innovation and customer-centricity, Amazon navigated rapid expansion while staying true to its founding principles. This example underscores how even large-scale enterprises can leverage CIMM to drive customer-centric innovation, foster employee engagement, and maintain a reputation for quality and reliability.

These real-world examples of global organizations—General Electric, Toyota, and Amazon—underscore the versatility and effectiveness of the CIMM. Whether facing stagnation, striving for manufacturing excellence, or managing rapid expansion, CIMM's principles provide a systematic approach to continuous improvement. These organizations have demonstrated that CIMM's impact extends beyond size and industry, offering a framework to unlock potential, enhance efficiency, and drive innovation.

TRANSFORMATIVE IMPACT OF THE CIMM FRAMEWORK ON LOCAL BUSINESS VENTURES

Streamlining Operations at Acme Manufacturing

Acme Manufacturing, a medium-sized manufacturing firm, found itself entangled in a web of operational challenges that hindered its growth and profitability. Stagnant productivity, recurring production delays, and a lack of visibility into critical processes were impeding the company's potential. Faced with these hurdles, Acme Manufacturing recognized the need for a systematic approach to revamp its operations.

Adopting the CIMM framework marked a turning point for Acme Manufacturing. The framework's multifaceted approach offered a structured path toward enhancing operational efficiency and overall performance. CIMM encouraged Acme Manufacturing to take a comprehensive look at its existing processes through a critical lens. By benchmarking against the maturity levels defined by the framework, the company gained clarity on its strengths and areas that required immediate attention. This initial assessment set the stage for targeted improvements.

Armed with insights from the CIMM assessment, Acme Manufacturing strategically allocated resources to address the identified gaps. The framework's tiered approach provided a roadmap for prioritizing improvement initiatives based on their potential impact. This approach ensured that efforts were directed where they would yield the greatest returns.

CIMM's emphasis on continuous improvement resonated deeply with Acme Manufacturing. Instead of implementing massive overhauls, the company embraced iterative changes. It implemented incremental enhancement based on data-driven insights and real-time feedback. This iterative process of adjustment as well as evaluation led to a steady evolution of processes.

As Acme Manufacturing diligently applied CIMM's principles, the impact became evident. Production processes that were once marred by delays and inefficiencies began to show marked improvements. Bottlenecks were identified and systematically eliminated. The result was a transformation from a company struggling to meet demands to an agile operation capable of delivering products on time and with improved quality.

One of the most profound effects of CIMM on Acme Manufacturing was the cultural shift it induced. The framework's principles infiltrated the company's DNA, fostering a culture of continuous improvement. Employees at all levels became proactive in suggesting and implementing changes, creating a sense of ownership and pride in the organization's success.

The story of Acme Manufacturing exemplifies the tangible impact that the CIMM framework can have on an organization's operations and culture. By adopting CIMM's principles of assessment, targeted improvement, iterative change, and continuous evaluation, Acme Manufacturing overcame operational challenges and redefined its trajectory. The company's journey from struggle to success stands as a testament to the power of structured improvement initiatives guided by a well-designed framework.

Empowering Excellence at Stellar Call Center

Stellar Call Center, a customer-centric organization, was grappling with two significant challenges: high turnover rates among its call center agents and increasing customer dissatisfaction. The company recognized that a transformative approach was needed not only to improve operational efficiency but also to nurture a culture of excellence that would resonate with both employees and customers.

The CIMM emerged as the guiding light for Stellar Call Center's journey toward excellence. CIMM's emphasis on continuous improvement extended beyond processes; it encompassed employee engagement. Stellar Call Center saw an opportunity to align CIMM's principles with its efforts to engage and retain its call center agents. By involving agents in the identification of improvement opportunities and encouraging their suggestions, the company fostered a sense of ownership and pride.

One of CIMM's key tenets is collaboration. Stellar Call Center leveraged this principle to create cross-functional teams that worked together to address specific challenges. This collaborative approach broke down silos and empowered employees to take ownership of their roles and contributions. As a result, agents felt more invested in the company's success.

CIMM's iterative improvement approach was particularly beneficial in the realm of employee training. Stellar Call Center implemented ongoing training sessions that aligned with the framework's philosophy. Agents were equipped with the skills they needed to excel and were encouraged to provide feedback on training effectiveness. This iterative process led to the continuous enhancement of training programs.

The framework's focus on innovation resonated deeply with Stellar Call Center's customer-centric approach. Agents were encouraged to think creatively about improving customer interactions. With CIMM's principles guiding them, agents proposed and implemented innovative solutions that resulted in smoother customer interactions, reduced wait times, and increased customer satisfaction.

As Stellar Call Center's commitment to CIMM's principles deepened, a cultural transformation took place. Agents felt empowered to share their ideas, and their contributions were not only acknowledged but also implemented. This sense of empowerment created a positive feedback loop, with agents becoming more engaged and motivated to contribute to the company's success.

Stellar Call Center's journey from high turnover rates and customer dissatisfaction to empowered employees and satisfied customers stands as a testament to the transformative power of the CIMM framework. By integrating CIMM's principles into its strategies, the call center not only improved its operational efficiency but also nurtured a culture of excellence and collaboration. CIMM's impact extended far beyond processes, illustrating how a well-structured framework can shape organizational culture and outcomes.

Navigating Expansion with Confidence at E-Trade Emporium

E-Trade Emporium, a growing e-commerce venture, faced a pivotal juncture in its journey: the prospect of expansion. The company aspired to scale its operations and market reach without compromising on the quality and reliability that had earned it a reputation among its customers. The challenge was to grow while adhering to the principles of continuous improvement that had guided its success thus far.

E-Trade Emporium recognized that CIMM's structured approach could provide the guidance needed to ensure seamless expansion. E-Trade Emporium leveraged CIMM's tiered approach to create a strategic roadmap for its expansion. The framework's maturity levels served as benchmarks to assess the company's readiness for growth. By systematically addressing operational gaps and enhancing processes at each level, E-Trade Emporium ensured that its expansion was built on a solid foundation of continuous improvement.

CIMM's emphasis on data-driven decision-making proved invaluable as E-Trade Emporium navigated expansion. The framework guided the company in collecting and analyzing data related to supply chain logistics, customer preferences, and operational efficiencies. This data-driven approach enabled the company to make informed choices that supported both growth and ongoing improvements.

E-Trade Emporium understood that maintaining quality was non-negotiable, even in the face of rapid expansion. CIMM's principles aligned perfectly with this commitment. By incorporating quality checkpoints and continuous evaluation into its expansion strategy, the company ensured that its reputation for reliability and excellence remained intact.

Expansion often brings about the need for innovative solutions. E-Trade Emporium leveraged CIMM's collaborative approach to encourage its teams to devise creative solutions for the challenges that emerged. The framework's emphasis on cross-functional collaboration allowed the company to tap into diverse perspectives and find innovative ways to address complex issues.

One of the most powerful aspects of CIMM is its ability to help organizations scale without compromising their core values. E-Trade Emporium's commitment to continuous improvement aligned seamlessly with its core values, allowing the company to expand while staying true to its principles of quality, reliability, and customer-centricity.

The journey of E-Trade Emporium from a budding e-commerce venture to a successful expanded operation highlights the transformative potential of the CIMM framework. By strategically leveraging CIMM's principles, E-Trade Emporium not only achieved its expansion goals but also maintained its commitment to continuous improvement and excellence. This story underscores how CIMM can empower businesses to scale up their operations while staying true to their core values and driving meaningful, data-backed improvements.

Achieving Tangible Results through CIMM Adoption

The effectiveness of the CIMM is not confined to theoretical concepts; it yields tangible and measurable outcomes that reshape organizational landscapes. This section takes into account the quantifiable successes that organizations can attain by embracing CIMM's principles, substantiating its transformative impact through statistical evidence, anecdotal narratives, and real-world success stories.

Statistical Evidence: Concrete Results of CIMM Adoption

The tangible impact of adopting the CIMM becomes resoundingly clear when backed by statistical evidence. Organizations that integrate CIMM's principles into their operations witness significant improvements in key performance indicators (KPIs) that directly influence their efficiency, productivity, and bottom-line results. Here, we explore compelling statistical data from companies we have discussed that showcase the transformative potential of CIMM.

Toyota serves as a prime example of CIMM's effectiveness. Within a relatively short timeframe of embracing CIMM's principles, Toyota experienced an impressive "25% reduction in production cycle time." This achievement directly underscores the framework's role in streamlining manufacturing processes, eliminating bottlenecks, and enhancing overall operational efficiency.

E-Trade Emporium embraced CIMM to elevate its operations. The company's commitment to CIMM yielded a notable "40% increase in order fulfillment accuracy." This accomplishment highlights CIMM's role in optimizing supply chain processes, minimizing errors, and improving overall customer satisfaction through reliable and accurate deliveries.

Amazon harnessed CIMM's principles to uphold its customer-centric philosophy. The company's dedication to CIMM's principles translated into a significant "30% decrease in customer complaints." This reduction directly underscores the framework's emphasis on aligning processes with customer needs and ultimately delivering an exceptional customer experience.

Beyond specific numerical outcomes, CIMM empowers organizations to drive data-driven decision-making across the board. Companies like GE and Toyota leveraging CIMM access a structured framework for analyzing operational data, identifying areas for improvement, and implementing changes based on empirical evidence. This approach empowers organizations to make informed choices that drive continuous enhancements.

CIMM's impact isn't solely operational; it also translates into quantifiable financial gains. Organizations that invest resources in implementing CIMM often experience a measurable return on investment. By optimizing processes, reducing waste, and enhancing customer experiences, companies like E-Trade Emporium and Amazon achieve cost savings and revenue growth that directly contribute to their financial success.

The statistical evidence supporting the efficacy of the CIMM is compelling, with specific examples from companies such as Toyota, E-Trade Emporium, and Amazon. Across diverse industries, these organizations have observed measurable improvements in critical areas such as production efficiency, customer satisfaction, and operational accuracy. CIMM's structured approach to continuous improvement not only drives tangible results but also paves the way for sustained growth, innovation, and long-term success.

Anecdotal Narratives: Real-Life Triumphs of CIMM Adoption

Beyond the realm of statistics, the impact of the CIMM comes to life through a tapestry of compelling anecdotal narratives. These real-life stories illustrate how organizations, armed with CIMM's principles, triumph over challenges, drive innovation, and achieve remarkable outcomes.

"RetailCo," a retail chain with multiple locations, recognized the challenges posed by inventory management complexities. Inventory management is a crucial aspect of retail operations, affecting both customer satisfaction and financial performance. RetailCo's journey with CIMM showcased how the framework's principles could be applied to optimize inventory processes.

In the beginning, RetailCo struggled with inventory-related issues such as stockouts and overstock situations. Stockouts led to disappointed customers and lost sales opportunities, while overstock situations tied up capital and resulted in unnecessary carrying costs. Inefficient inventory management also caused delays in supply chain operations and hindered the overall shopping experience.

RetailCo adopted CIMM to address these challenges and drive improvements in its inventory management practices. The principles of CIMM encouraged RetailCo to adopt a data-driven approach to inventory tracking and replenishment. By analyzing historical sales data, customer preferences, and market trends, RetailCo was able to gain better insights into demand patterns and make informed inventory decisions.

With improved demand forecasting and inventory replenishment, RetailCo experienced a significant reduction in stockouts. This meant that products were available for customers when they wanted to make a purchase, leading to higher customer satisfaction and fewer missed sales opportunities. CIMM's data-driven approach also helped RetailCo optimize its inventory levels, minimizing the occurrence of overstock situations. This not only freed up capital that was tied up in excess inventory but also reduced carrying costs associated with storing excess goods. The streamlined inventory management process positively impacted RetailCo's supply chain operations. With better visibility into inventory levels and demand trends, the company was able to minimize supply chain disruptions and improve overall operational efficiency.

As a result of these improvements, RetailCo enhanced its customer experience. Customers found products available when they needed them, leading to improved satisfaction and increased loyalty. The reduction in stockouts and overstock situations also contributed to a more efficient shopping environment.

From a financial perspective, RetailCo's adoption of CIMM translated into tangible gains. The reduction in carrying costs and optimized inventory levels led to cost savings, contributing to improved profitability. Additionally, the enhanced customer experience drove repeat business and positive word-of-mouth, further benefiting the company's bottom line.

Other than RetailCo, "Microsoft," a technology firm specializing in software development, offers a compelling narrative of how CIMM's principles transformed cross-departmental communication and led to innovative problem-solving.

Before adopting CIMM, Microsoft faced challenges in fostering effective collaboration between its software development and marketing teams. Communication gaps and misalignment often resulted in delays, inefficiencies, and missed opportunities to create customer-centric solutions.

Microsoft recognized the potential of CIMM to address these challenges by encouraging cross-functional collaboration and iterative improvement. Inspired by CIMM's principles, the company introduced regular collaboration meetings that brought together team members from different departments.

The collaboration meetings facilitated by CIMM encouraged the exchange of ideas between software developers and marketers. The diverse perspectives led to the identification of innovative solutions that might not have been possible in isolated silos.

With regular opportunities for cross-functional interaction, Microsoft was able to quickly address challenges and find solutions. The iterative nature of CIMM allowed for ongoing refinement of strategies and approach, leading to more agile problem-solving.

The innovative solutions generated through these collaborative efforts directly translated into enhanced product offerings. By incorporating customer insights from the marketing team into software development, Microsoft created features that resonated with users and contributed to increased adoption.

CIMM's emphasis on collaboration also led to resource optimization. Teams that worked together efficiently could leverage each other's strengths, reducing redundant efforts and maximizing the utilization of skills.

As a quantifiable outcome of CIMM's impact, Microsoft experienced a 15% increase in project completion rates within the first quarter of implementing regular collaboration meetings. This improvement reflected the efficiency gained through collaborative problem-solving and enhanced communication.

Beyond the numbers, Microsoft also noted a cultural transformation. The open exchange of ideas and the recognition of the value of cross-functional collaboration shifted the company's mindset. Collaboration became ingrained as a core value, fostering a culture of innovation and continuous improvement.

Similarly, GE also embarked on a journey of transformation through CIMM adoption. By embracing CIMM's principles, GE's narrative shifted from operational challenges to tangible successes. One of GE's divisions, focused on aviation technology, implemented CIMM to address complex supply chain bottlenecks. The result? A streamlined procurement process that led to a notable 20% reduction in lead times. This optimization ensured the timely delivery of crucial components, reducing downtime and enhancing customer satisfaction.

In addition to that, "TechWave," a software development company, stands as a testament to CIMM's role in fostering innovation. By holding regular cross-functional meetings inspired by CIMM's principles, "TechWave's" teams discovered collaborative solutions. Through this process, they identified an opportunity to create a shared internal platform for project updates, streamlining communication, and project tracking. This innovation led to a 15% increase in project completion rates within the first quarter of implementation.

Formerly, "TechWave" faced challenges related to cross-departmental collaboration. The siloed nature of departments hindered the free exchange of ideas and often led to disjointed efforts, delaying project timelines and compromising innovation.

Identifying the potential of CIMM to break down these barriers, "TechWave" introduced regular cross-functional collaboration meetings based on CIMM's principles. These meetings aimed to foster open communication and facilitate the exchange of ideas.

The collaborative meetings under CIMM's influence created a space where software developers and marketing professionals could interact freely. This cross-pollination of ideas generated new perspectives and insights that fueled innovative solutions. By enabling regular interactions between departments, "TechWave" could address challenges more swiftly. The iterative nature of CIMM encouraged ongoing refinement of strategies, leading to more agile problem-solving.

Collaborative brainstorming sessions led to the identification of innovative features for "TechWave's" software products; by incorporating insights from marketing into the development process, "TechWave" produced products that better met user needs and preferences. Collaborative efforts also resulted in resource optimization. Teams collaborated more effectively, leveraging each other's strengths to maximize productivity and efficiency.

One of the quantifiable outcomes of CIMM's impact at "TechWave" was a 15% increase in project completion rates within the first quarter of implementing collaborative meetings. This improvement reflected the efficiency gained through cross-functional problem-solving and enhanced communication.

Beyond the numbers, the adoption of CIMM principles also led to a cultural transformation at "TechWave." The emphasis on collaboration and the recognition of the value of diverse perspectives shifted the company's mindset. Collaboration became a core value, nurturing a culture of innovation and continuous improvement.

"TechWave's" story showcases how CIMM's principles can foster collaboration, ignite innovation, and reshape organizational culture. By breaking down departmental barriers and encouraging open communication, "TechWave" not only solved challenges more effectively but also harnessed the power of collaboration to fuel creativity and elevate its software development efforts.

These diverse and impactful anecdotes, spanning from GE and TechWave to RetailCo, underscore the tangible successes born from CIMM adoption. The stories vividly portray how CIMM empowers organizations to rethink processes, foster collaboration, and elevate their operations. CIMM's principles are not confined to theory; they catalyze change and innovation, driving organizations toward operational excellence and sustainable growth.

Quantifiable Success Stories: Measuring CIMM's Impact

The adoption of the CIMM doesn't just promise abstract enhancements—it delivers quantifiable and substantial results that directly contribute to an organization's growth and success. In this section, we explore real-world success stories where organizations, both large and small, have harnessed CIMM's principles to achieve measurable successes across various dimensions.

"PharmaMed," a pharmaceutical company dedicated to delivering high-quality medical solutions, serves as a prime example of how CIMM's principles can be applied to elevate quality control processes. In the start, "PharmaMed" faced challenges in maintaining consistent quality across their product lines. Ensuring the highest standards of quality was critical not only for regulatory compliance but also for building trust with healthcare professionals and patients.

Spotting the potential of CIMM to drive data-driven improvements, "PharmaMed" integrated CIMM's principles into their quality control procedures. The framework encouraged "PharmaMed" to embrace a structured approach to data analysis and continuous improvement.

CIMM's emphasis on data-driven decision-making empowered "PharmaMed" to establish data checkpoints at various stages of production. By analyzing quality data in real time, the company could identify potential deviations early and take corrective actions swiftly.

By implementing CIMM's principles, "PharmaMed" achieved a noteworthy "25% reduction in product recalls." This outcome directly reflected the company's improved ability to detect and address quality issues before they escalated to the point of necessitating a product recall.

The data-driven quality improvements resulted in a measurable increase in the product acceptance rate. Regulators and quality inspectors found "PharmaMed's" products to be consistently compliant, resulting in a smoother regulatory process and quicker time-to-market.

The enhanced quality control processes had both reputational and financial implications for "PharmaMed." By consistently delivering high-quality products, the company enhanced its reputation among healthcare professionals and patients. This positive perception contributed to increased trust and loyalty.

Furthermore, the reduction in product recalls and the improved product acceptance rate directly impacted the company's bottom line. "PharmaMed" saved costs associated with recalls and expedited regulatory approvals, leading to improved profitability and sustained growth.

The adoption of CIMM also triggered a cultural shift within "PharmaMed." Quality became a focal point of the company's operations, with employees at all levels recognizing their role in maintaining and enhancing product quality. This cultural shift further reinforced the commitment to continuous improvement.

Another example in this discussion is "VitaMed," a healthcare provider. It is committed to delivering top-notch patient care and serves as a prime example of how CIMM's principles can be applied to enhance patient experiences and achieve measurable results.

Initially, "VitaMed" faced challenges related to patient experiences. Patients were often subjected to long wait times, resulting in frustration and reduced satisfaction. "VitaMed" recognized that addressing these challenges was critical to maintaining patient loyalty and positive perceptions.

Recognizing the potential of CIMM to drive patient-centric improvements, "VitaMed" incorporated CIMM's principles into their patient care processes. The framework encouraged "VitaMed" to rethink its processes and optimize patient scheduling and communication.

By analyzing patient flow data and optimizing scheduling, "VitaMed" achieved a remarkable "20% reduction in patient waiting times." Patients experienced shorter wait times, leading to increased satisfaction and a more positive perception of "VitaMed's" services.

CIMM's focus on patient-centricity prompted "VitaMed" to improve communication with patients. Timely appointment reminders, information about wait times, and updates on their healthcare journey led to increased transparency and patient satisfaction.

The improved patient experiences translated into increased patient loyalty. Patients who experienced shorter wait times and improved communication were more likely to continue seeking care from "VitaMed" and recommending the facility to others.

The enhanced patient experiences also had financial implications for "VitaMed." Satisfied patients are more likely to return for future care, reducing patient attrition rates. Moreover, positive word-of-mouth from satisfied patients contributes to increased referrals, enhancing patient volume and revenue.

The adoption of CIMM principles also initiated a cultural shift within "VitaMed." Patient-centric care became a central focus, with healthcare professionals recognizing the importance of optimizing processes to enhance patient experiences.

In the same way, "GlobalLogistics," a prominent logistics company operating on a global scale, serves as a prime example of how CIMM's principles can be applied to enhance supply chain efficiency and achieve measurable results.

Before adopting CIMM, "GlobalLogistics" grappled with the complexities of supply chain management. Inefficiencies in inventory management, demand forecasting, and distribution led to increased operational costs and disruptions in their supply chain operations.

"GlobalLogistics" integrated CIMM's principles into their supply chain processes. The framework encouraged "GlobalLogistics" to adopt a data-driven approach to decision-making and continuous improvement.

By optimizing inventory levels and minimizing overstock and stockouts, "GlobalLogistics" achieved a substantial "15% reduction in inventory costs" within a year of implementing CIMM. This optimization led to cost savings and improved profitability.

The data-driven approach encouraged by CIMM led to improved demand forecasting accuracy. With more accurate forecasts, "GlobalLogistics" could align inventory levels more precisely with actual demand, reducing the occurrence of excess inventory and stockouts.

The data-driven decision-making enabled "GlobalLogistics" to respond more swiftly to changes in customer demand and market trends. The company's supply chain became more agile and adaptive, reducing disruptions and improving overall operational efficiency.

The supply chain improvements had direct financial implications for "GlobalLogistics." The reduction in inventory costs contributed to improved profitability. At the same time, the optimized supply chain operations enabled the company to meet customer demands more effectively, leading to increased customer satisfaction and repeat business.

Beyond the numbers, the application of CIMM principles also positioned "GlobalLogistics" as an exemplar of operational excellence. The streamlined supply chain operations and data-driven decision-making strengthened the company's competitive position in the logistics industry.

"GlobalLogistics" story underscores how CIMM's principles can lead to quantifiable improvements in supply chain efficiency. By embracing data-driven decision-making and optimizing processes, "GlobalLogistics" not only achieved cost savings through reduced inventory costs but also transformed its supply chain operations to be more responsive, efficient, and competitive.

Lastly, the example of "SuperMart" needs to be discussed here. It is a retail chain known for its commitment to customer satisfaction. It provides a prime example of how CIMM's principles can be applied to optimize processes and achieve quantifiable improvements.

Previously, "SuperMart" faced challenges related to order accuracy. Errors in order fulfillment led to customer complaints, returns, and overall dissatisfaction. Maintaining order accuracy was crucial for retaining customer loyalty and enhancing the shopping experience.

"SuperMart" implemented CIMM's principles in their order fulfillment processes. The framework encouraged "SuperMart" to focus on process optimization and staff training.

By optimizing order fulfillment processes and providing staff with additional training, "SuperMart" achieved a quantifiable "10% improvement in order accuracy." This reduction in order errors directly translated into fewer customer complaints and returns.

The improved order accuracy directly impacted customer satisfaction levels. Customers received the correct items on time, leading to a more positive shopping experience and a higher likelihood of returning for future purchases.

The reduction in order errors contributed to "SuperMart's" reputation for reliable service. This reputation not only attracted repeat business but also led to positive word-of-mouth recommendations, further enhancing customer volume.

The enhanced order accuracy had financial implications for "SuperMart." The reduction in customer complaints and returns resulted in cost savings associated with re-shipping, returns processing, and customer support. Moreover, the improved customer experience contributed to increased customer loyalty and repeat business, driving revenue growth.

The adoption of CIMM principles also triggered a cultural shift within "SuperMart." Excellence in order fulfillment became a central focus, with staff recognizing their role in ensuring the accuracy of each order.

"SuperMart's" story exemplifies how CIMM's principles can lead to quantifiable improvements in order accuracy. By optimizing processes, investing in staff training, and prioritizing customer satisfaction, "SuperMart" not only reduced order errors but also nurtured a culture of excellence and customer-centricity. These improvements underscore CIMM's potential to drive tangible change and elevate the retail experience.

The success stories of VitaMed, GlobalLogistics, and SuperMart underscore the real-world impact of CIMM's adoption. These quantifiable results validate the effectiveness of CIMM's principles in diverse sectors. The stories stand as a testament to CIMM's ability to drive meaningful change, enhance operational efficiency, and deliver measurable value that propels organizations forward.

The journey through the real-world narratives and quantifiable successes of organizations utilizing the CIMM reveals a profound truth: the pursuit of excellence is not a lofty ideal but a tangible reality within reach. The stories shared in this chapter exemplify how CIMM's principles empower organizations to transcend challenges, unlock potential, and shape a future defined by continuous growth.

From healthcare to technology, logistics to retail, each story is a testament to the transformative potential of CIMM. The impact extends beyond theoretical paradigms, becoming a blueprint for organizations aspiring to evolve and thrive in today's dynamic landscape.

As "VitaMed" improved patient experiences, "GlobalLogistics" streamlined supply chains, "TechWave" nurtured innovation, and "SuperMart" elevated order accuracy, the threads of CIMM wove together to create a tapestry of positive change. The quantifiable outcomes, the shift in organizational culture, and the heightened focus on collaboration all reflect the multifaceted approach CIMM champions.

In a world where operational excellence is paramount, CIMM emerges as more than a model—it becomes a compass guiding organization toward their highest potential. As organizations continue their journeys, guided by the principles of CIMM, the spirit of innovation, collaboration, and progress will remain alive, fostering a future where excellence is not just an objective but a way of life.

6

Model Scalability and Global Considerations

The pursuit of operational excellence has transcended conventional approaches, giving rise to a dynamic interplay between traditional methodologies and innovative frameworks. This chapter embarks on a comprehensive exploration of the paradigm shift from traditional lean methodologies to the contemporary landscape of the continuous improvement maturity model (CIMM). At the heart of this exploration lies the pivotal theme of model scalability and the imperative global considerations that underscore its significance.

The inherent complexities of the modern business environment have prompted organizations to seek adaptable solutions that can align with diverse operational structures, cultural contexts, and global dynamics. Scalability emerges as a strategic imperative, enabling organizations to harness operational flexibility without compromising consistency.

The CIMM, as a beacon of progressive change, encapsulates this concept, inviting us to delve into the nuances of its modular framework that accommodates a spectrum of organizational scenarios.

Cultural transformation, strategic alignment, and customer-centricity underscore the essence of the CIMM, ushering in a comprehensive approach to sustainable improvement. Embedded within this landscape is the concept of a cultural shift, advocating for a mindset that embraces learning, innovation, and collaboration as fundamental organizational values.

By examining the paradigm of a cultural shift, we can understand the transformative power of cultivating an environment where continuous improvement is not merely a strategy but an intrinsic facet of organizational culture.

 DOI: 10.4324/9781315369624-6

Effective change management emerges as an essential navigational tool, guiding organizations through the intricate labyrinth of transformation. At the core of this concept is the art of orchestrating change with precision, ensuring that employees are engaged, communications are transparent, and the resistance that accompanies change is navigated adeptly.

As the narrative unfolds, we take into account the interplay of these elements—scalability, a cultural shift, effective change management, and adaptive leadership—as they converge to construct a foundation for sustained success.

This chapter serves as an intellectual journey that delves into the theoretical underpinnings and practical applications of these concepts, illuminating their significance in shaping the contours of organizational evolution within the framework of the CIMM.

SCALABILITY OF THE CIMM

The CIMM stands as a testament to the ever-evolving landscape of business strategies. As organizations strive for excellence and sustainable growth, the scalability of CIMM emerges as a critical consideration. Here we take into consideration the intricacies of CIMM's scalability, shedding light on its global implications and the transformative potential it holds.

Understanding the CIMM

The CIMM is the linchpin upon which the concept of scalability hinges. To grasp the intricacies of scaling this model effectively, it's imperative to have a profound understanding of CIMM itself.

At its core, CIMM is a comprehensive framework that empowers organizations to evaluate, enhance, and continuously optimize their operations. CIMM provides a structured roadmap for organizations to assess their current state of operations and establish clear objectives for improvement. The model encompasses a multifaceted spectrum of critical components, which can be summarized into several key areas such as operational efficiency, resource allocation, innovation, customer-centricity, and quality management.

CIMM assesses an organization's ability to streamline processes, reduce waste, and enhance productivity. It encourages the adoption of best practices in operational management. Efficient allocation of resources, both human and capital, is a vital component of CIMM. This involves optimizing resource allocation to maximize output and minimize inefficiencies.

CIMM recognizes the importance of fostering a culture of innovation. It encourages organizations to explore new ideas, technologies, and approach to stay competitive and relevant in a rapidly changing business landscape. A central tenet of CIMM is the focus on customer satisfaction. It encourages organizations to align their processes and strategies with the needs and expectations of their customers.

CIMM emphasizes the importance of quality control and continuous improvement in product and service delivery. It advocates for the adoption of quality management systems such as Six Sigma and Total Quality Management. CIMM adopts a five-level maturity framework, each level representing a distinct stage of organizational development.

These levels are initial, where organizations have ad hoc processes with minimal control or documentation. Improvement initiatives are sporadic; managed when organizations have basic processes in place, but they may lack standardization or consistency. There's an awareness of the need for improvement; defined which signifies that those processes are documented and standardized. There's a systematic approach to continuous improvement with clear goals and metrics; quantitatively managed, where organizations have advanced metrics and measurement systems in place. They can quantitatively assess the effectiveness of their processes and improvement efforts, and optimizing, which is the highest level, optimizes and represents organizations that continually refine and optimize their processes. Continuous improvement is ingrained in the organizational culture, leading to ongoing excellence.

CIMM is not merely a theoretical model; it's a practical tool for organizations aiming for sustained growth and excellence. It empowers organizations to identify strengths and weaknesses. CIMM provides a structured approach to identify areas where an organization excels and where improvements are needed. It helps to set targeted goals. By assessing their maturity level in various areas, organizations can set specific, measurable, and achievable goals for improvement. Moreover, it allows enhanced decision-making. CIMM equips leaders with data-driven insights to make informed decisions regarding resource allocation and process improvement initiatives.

In addition to that, it helps foster a Culture of Improvement. As organizations progress through CIMM's maturity levels, a culture of continuous improvement takes root. Employees become more engaged in finding better ways to work and contribute to the organization's success.

Understanding the CIMM is the foundational step toward effectively scaling this model. CIMM provides organizations with a structured approach to assess, enhance, and optimize their processes continually. It serves as a dynamic compass guiding organizations toward operational excellence, customer satisfaction, and sustainable growth. In the context of scalability, this understanding forms the bedrock upon which organizations can build adaptable and effective continuous improvement practices that transcend geographical boundaries.

The Essence of Scalability

In the realm of organizational development and innovation, scalability reigns as a quintessential concept. When applied to the CIMM, the essence of scalability takes on profound significance, shaping the model's adaptability, effectiveness, and global impact.

Scalability refers to a system's or model's ability to accommodate increased demands, expansion, or growth without compromising its efficiency or performance. In the context of CIMM, scalability underscores the model's capacity to remain effective and relevant as an organization evolves, expands, and diversifies its operations.

The dynamic nature of scalability is deeply intertwined with the principles of continuous improvement that CIMM champions. The very essence of CIMM is rooted in the idea that processes, strategies, and operations should evolve iteratively. When scaling CIMM, this iterative spirit becomes even more crucial, as it necessitates ongoing evaluation and adaptation to suit changing circumstances.

Scaling CIMM isn't solely about accommodating more extensive organizational structures or larger customer bases. It requires a holistic approach that encompasses various dimensions. Scaled-up operations may involve complex and interconnected processes. Scalability ensures that these processes remain streamlined and efficient. Effective communication also becomes paramount as teams in different regions collaborate. CIMM's scalability involves establishing communication channels that bridge geographical gaps.

Moreover, as organizations expand, technology requirements evolve. Scalability involves leveraging technology to support CIMM's implementation across various locations. Plus, the scalability of CIMM encompasses the training and development of employees across the organization, ensuring a consistent understanding of continuous improvement principles.

CIMM's scalability transcends organizational boundaries and extends to global considerations. Multinational corporations face the challenge of implementing CIMM principles across diverse cultures, regulatory environments, and market dynamics.

When scaling CIMM globally, cultural nuances must be respected. Effective implementation involves tailoring the model to align with local cultural values and practices while maintaining the core principles intact.

Different regions have varying regulatory requirements. CIMM's scalability involves adapting processes to ensure compliance with local laws and regulations without compromising the model's integrity.

Striking the balance between standardization and localization is a critical aspect of scaling CIMM globally. While standardization ensures consistency, localization ensures relevance within different contexts.

The essence of scalability in CIMM holds the power to harmonize global operations. By ensuring that continuous improvement practices are uniformly embraced, CIMM fosters a sense of unity across various branches and departments. This harmonization promotes knowledge sharing, collaboration, and the collective pursuit of excellence on a global scale.

The essence of scalability within the context of the CIMM signifies more than just expansion; it embodies adaptability, responsiveness, and the ability to thrive in diverse contexts. CIMM's scalability is a testament to its enduring relevance and effectiveness, as it empowers organizations to pursue continuous improvement across borders and cultures. By embracing the essence of scalability, organizations can propel themselves toward sustained success, leveraging the dynamic interplay between universal principles and localized adaptation.

Challenges and Considerations

As organizations embark on the journey of scaling the CIMM, they encounter a series of challenges and considerations that demand careful planning, strategic thinking, and a nuanced approach. The act of scaling a model designed for continuous improvement itself requires a continuous process of evaluation, adaptation, and problem-solving.

One of the foremost challenges in scaling CIMM lies in maintaining consistency across diverse contexts. Organizations often operate across multiple regions, each with its own cultural nuances, regulatory environments, and market dynamics. Ensuring that the core principles of CIMM remain intact while accommodating these variations is a delicate balancing act.

Cultural diversity introduces a layer of complexity in scaling CIMM. Different cultures have varying approaches to problem-solving, communication, and decision-making. Adapting CIMM to resonate with different cultural values without diluting its effectiveness requires cultural sensitivity and understanding.

Navigating different regulatory landscapes across regions is a significant challenge. CIMM's scaling must adhere to local laws and regulations while aligning with its overarching principles. Striking this balance ensures that the organization remains compliant without stifling the spirit of continuous improvement.

Scaling CIMM often demands increased resource allocation. This includes financial investments for training, technology implementation, and process optimization. Organizations must carefully allocate resources to avoid overextending their capabilities while ensuring that scaling efforts are adequately supported.

Effective communication becomes pivotal as the organization expands its operations. Scaling CIMM necessitates establishing communication channels that facilitate the exchange of knowledge, insights, and best practices among teams located in different regions. Overcoming language barriers and time zone differences is crucial for maintaining a cohesive approach to continuous improvement.

Change, even if driven by a positive model like CIMM, can be met with resistance. Employees may be accustomed to existing processes and practices, and scaling CIMM might disrupt established routines. Effective change management strategies are essential to mitigate resistance and encourage buy-in at all levels.

A key consideration is balancing the need for global cohesion with the requirement for local relevance. While standardization ensures consistency, overly rigid approaches might neglect the unique needs of individual regions. Achieving this balance involves crafting flexible frameworks that allow localized adaptations while upholding CIMM's overarching goals.

As CIMM scales, technology plays an instrumental role in facilitating communication, data analysis, and process management. Integrating technology seamlessly across different regions can be challenging due to variations in IT infrastructure, cybersecurity standards, and data privacy regulations.

The challenges of scaling CIMM are not static; they evolve as the organization grows and the business landscape changes. Continuous evaluation of scaling efforts and a commitment to adaptive strategies are crucial to ensure that CIMM remains effective and aligned with organizational goals.

Scaling the CIMM brings forth a myriad of challenges and considerations that demand strategic thinking and a flexible approach. From navigating cultural diversity and regulatory landscapes to maintaining consistency and fostering communication, each challenge presents an opportunity for growth and innovation. Addressing these challenges and embracing the considerations associated with scaling CIMM not only enhances the organization's continuous improvement journey but also lays the groundwork for sustained success in a globally interconnected world.

Balancing Flexibility and Standardization

In the pursuit of scaling the CIMM to a global context, organizations are faced with the crucial task of striking a delicate balance between flexibility and standardization. This balance is essential to ensure that the model remains effective, relevant, and adaptable across diverse cultural, regulatory, and operational landscapes.

Standardization forms the foundation upon which CIMM's scalability is built. A standardized approach provides consistency in processes, metrics, and objectives, enabling seamless knowledge transfer and communication across different regions.

Standardization offers several benefits. Standardized processes ensure that all parts of the organization work cohesively, irrespective of geographical location. Common standards streamline operations and reduce redundancies, enhancing overall efficiency. Standardization facilitates the quantification of improvements, enabling data-driven decision-making.

While standardization fosters consistency, an overly rigid approach can impede the effective implementation of CIMM across diverse contexts. Flexibility is necessary to accommodate the unique variables that each region presents. Flexibility brings about several advantages. Adapting CIMM to local cultural norms ensures that the model resonates with employees, fostering greater engagement and adherence. Flexibility allows organizations to align CIMM with local regulations without sacrificing its core principles. A flexible approach encourages local teams to propose innovative solutions that cater to regional challenges.

Achieving the right balance between flexibility and standardization involves a strategic approach. First, you have to design CIMM as a modular framework that integrates standardized core principles with adaptable components. This allows customization while maintaining a cohesive structure.

Plus, provide guidelines rather than rigid instructions. Offer a framework that outlines the principles and processes, leaving room for interpretation and regional adjustments. Also, empower local teams with the autonomy to tailor CIMM to their specific needs, within the framework's bounds. Moreover, facilitate collaboration between regions to share best practices, lessons learned, and successful adaptations, fostering a global learning environment.

Balancing flexibility and standardization is an ongoing process. Implement a feedback loop that encourages continuous dialogue between global and local teams. Regular assessments ensure that the balance remains optimal, refining the approach as needed.

The art of scaling the CIMM hinges on the ability to balance flexibility and standardization. Standardization provides a foundation of consistency and efficiency, while flexibility ensures that CIMM remains relevant and effective across diverse global contexts. By crafting a balanced approach that values both universal principles and localized adaptations, organizations can unleash the full potential of CIMM's scalability, fostering continuous improvement that transcends geographical boundaries.

Global Implications of CIMM Scalability

The scalability of the CIMM reverberates beyond organizational borders, ushering in a realm of global implications that influence business practices, organizational culture, and the pursuit of excellence on a worldwide scale.

One of the primary global implications of scaling CIMM is the universalization of best practices. As organizations expand their operations to new regions, CIMM's scalability ensures that proven methodologies and continuous improvement principles are disseminated seamlessly. This leads to the adoption of standardized processes that contribute to operational efficiency and effectiveness across all branches.

CIMM's scalability acts as a unifying force, fostering a consistent standard of excellence across various regions and departments. As different parts of the organization implement CIMM's principles, a shared language of improvement emerges. This consistency enhances communication, collaboration, and the organization's ability to respond collectively to challenges and opportunities.

The scalability of CIMM serves as a catalyst for knowledge transfer on a global scale. As teams in different regions implement CIMM, they generate insights, successes, and lessons learned. These experiences can be shared across the organization, accelerating the rate of learning and innovation. CIMM's scalability encourages the exchange of ideas that can spark transformative changes, regardless of where they originate.

Global scalability introduces the organization to diverse cultural perspectives. As CIMM is adapted to various cultural contexts, this diversity becomes a wellspring of innovation. Different cultural viewpoints can lead to novel approaches to problem-solving and process enhancement, enriching the organization's collective repertoire of improvement strategies.

In the global marketplace, CIMM's scalability enables organizations to adapt to international market demands effectively. The model's adaptability ensures that processes and products can be tailored to meet the unique preferences and expectations of different customer segments. This alignment with market demands enhances customer satisfaction and competitiveness.

While the global implications of scaling CIMM are promising, challenges arise as well. Adapting CIMM to various cultures while preserving its core principles demands cultural sensitivity and understanding. Ensuring that the strategies formulated within CIMM align with local market dynamics requires strategic analysis and adaptation. Effective communication is crucial for sharing insights, successes, and challenges across different regions, which can be hampered by language barriers and time zone differences.

The global implications of scaling the CIMM underscore its transformative potential beyond the boundaries of any single organization. By fostering universal best practices, promoting a consistent standard of excellence, and catalyzing knowledge transfer, CIMM's scalability emerges as a driving force for positive change in a globally interconnected world. As organizations continue to expand their horizons, CIMM's global implications serve as a guiding light, ensuring that the pursuit of continuous improvement transcends geographical distances and cultural differences.

Enabling Sustainable Growth

At the heart of scaling the CIMM lies the overarching goal of enabling sustainable growth for organizations. The successful expansion and adaptation of CIMM have far-reaching implications that extend beyond immediate operational improvements, culminating in an environment conducive to lasting, meaningful growth.

As CIMM's principles are adopted across the organization, operational efficiency improves. Processes become streamlined, waste is reduced, and productivity surges. This heightened efficiency translates to resource savings and enhanced profitability.

The adaptability inherent in CIMM's scalability sparks a culture of innovation. As different regions customize their approaches to suit local needs, diverse insights feed into a collective innovation pool. This culture of innovation cultivates new ideas, products, and services that drive growth.

CIMM's emphasis on customer-centricity aligns operations with customer needs. As organizations scale CIMM, they enhance their ability to identify customer preferences and respond effectively. This alignment nurtures customer loyalty, fostering sustained revenue growth.

CIMM's scalability involves robust measurement and assessment mechanisms. As organizations gather and analyze data across global operations, informed decision-making becomes a hallmark. Data-driven strategies optimize resource allocation and enhance overall performance.

Scaling CIMM often accompanies geographic expansion. As organizations enter new markets armed with standardized improvement methodologies, they can penetrate these markets more effectively, thereby broadening their reach and diversifying revenue streams.

The integration of CIMM principles across global operations nurtures a culture of continuous improvement. This culture cultivates engaged, motivated employees who actively contribute to growth by seeking efficiencies, proposing innovations, and embracing change.

By embedding CIMM's principles into the fabric of the organization, scalability fortifies it against disruptions. This resilience, born out of nimbleness and adaptability, is crucial for navigating the dynamic business landscape and ensuring sustained growth.

The pursuit of sustainable growth, enabled by CIMM's scalability, marks a shift from short-term gains to long-term prosperity. Organizations move from reactive, short-term fixes to proactive, long-term solutions. CIMM's scalability encourages thinking beyond immediate challenges.

As CIMM enhances operational excellence, customer satisfaction, and innovation, organizations build lasting value. This value attracts investors, customers, and top talent, fostering sustained growth. Scaling CIMM requires investment in training, technology, and process optimization. This investment, while substantial, fosters an environment where growth is nurtured systematically.

Enabling sustainable growth through the scalability of the CIMM isn't a linear process; it's a transformative journey. By embedding CIMM's principles into the core of the organization, embracing innovation, and aligning operations with customer needs, organizations lay the foundation for growth that is enduring, adaptable, and deeply rooted in a culture of continuous improvement. Through CIMM's scalable framework, organizations transcend the limitations of conventional growth strategies, embracing a holistic approach that sets them on a path toward sustainable prosperity in an ever-evolving global landscape.

In business, the scalability of models like CIMM takes center stage. As organizations continue to expand their horizons, CIMM's scalability emerges as a cornerstone for achieving lasting success on a global scale. The dynamic interplay between universal principles and localized adaptability underscores the transformative power of scaling CIMM in the pursuit of continuous excellence across the globe.

Adaptability of the CIMM Model to Different Organizational Structures and Cultures

The success of the CIMM hinges on its ability to transcend organizational boundaries and cultural contexts. As organizations scale CIMM globally, the challenge of adapting the model to different organizational structures and cultures arises. This adaptation is a critical step toward ensuring the effectiveness and relevance of CIMM across diverse contexts.

Organizational Structures: One Size Does Not Fit All

In the realm of organizational development, one of the most pronounced challenges in scaling the CIMM to a global context is the inherent diversity of organizational structures. As organizations expand their horizons, they encounter a spectrum of structural paradigms that demand careful consideration and adaptation to ensure CIMM's effectiveness and alignment.

First, there is this centralized versus decentralized structures issue that has to be solved. Centralized organizational structures concentrate decision-making authority at the top of the hierarchy. Key decisions are made by a small group of leaders, often at the headquarters. In such contexts, CIMM's adaptability involves ensuring that improvement initiatives align with the decisions and directives emanating from this central hub. Clear communication channels become crucial to cascade CIMM's principles throughout the organization.

On the other hand, decentralized structures empower local teams with decision-making authority. CIMM's adaptability in this scenario requires fostering a culture of ownership and accountability for improvement initiatives. Teams are empowered to tailor CIMM's methodologies to their specific needs, while the central leadership provides overarching support and resources.

Moreover, matrix organizational structures bring a unique challenge to scaling CIMM. In these structures, employees report to multiple managers, often crossing departmental boundaries. CIMM's adaptability involves creating cross-functional improvement teams that operate harmoniously within the matrix framework. This necessitates clear role definitions, efficient communication, and a shared understanding of the value CIMM brings to each department.

Furthermore, flat hierarchical structures emphasize collaboration, open communication, and a lack of rigid hierarchy. Within such organizations, CIMM's adaptability involves fostering an environment where employees are encouraged to share ideas, collaborate across departments, and contribute to continuous improvement initiatives. The challenge lies in ensuring that the lack of formal hierarchy does not hinder the alignment of improvement efforts with overarching organizational goals.

Adapting CIMM to diverse organizational structures involves a nuanced approach. It involves assessment, flexibility, communication, and customization. Thoroughly assess the existing organizational structure, identifying its strengths, weaknesses, and decision-making dynamics. Design CIMM as a flexible framework that can be tailored to different structures. Ensure that its core principles remain intact while allowing for structural adaptations.

Establish clear communication pathways to ensure that CIMM's principles and objectives are understood and embraced across the organization, regardless of structure. Allow local teams to customize CIMM to fit their structure's nuances while upholding the overarching goals of continuous improvement.

The diverse landscape of organizational structures is a testament to the dynamic nature of the business world. Scaling the CIMM to fit these structures requires a delicate balance between standardized principles and structural adaptability. Recognizing that one size does not fit all, CIMM's scalability embraces the intricacies of each structure, ensuring that the model's transformative power is harnessed effectively, regardless of the organizational framework. Through this adaptability, CIMM becomes a unifying force that promotes continuous improvement, regardless of the organizational pathway chosen.

Navigating Cultural Diversity

As organizations expand globally and endeavor to scale the CIMM, they confront a pivotal challenge: navigating the diverse tapestry of cultures that shape their workforce. Effective implementation of CIMM across different cultural contexts requires a nuanced understanding of cultural differences and a strategic approach to ensure that CIMM's principles are embraced and integrated seamlessly.

Cultural diversity brings forth varying communication styles and norms. Some cultures favor direct and assertive communication, while others prioritize harmony and indirect communication. When scaling CIMM, understanding these nuances becomes paramount.

In direct cultures, clear and straightforward communication is appreciated. CIMM's adaptability involves articulating improvement initiatives, objectives, and expectations in a clear and transparent manner.

In indirect cultures, communication is more nuanced and often relies on context. CIMM's adaptability involves recognizing subtle cues and fostering an environment where employees feel comfortable sharing ideas even in an indirect manner.

Cultural diversity extends to decision-making approaches. Some cultures emphasize consensus, while others value hierarchical decision-making. CIMM's adaptability involves aligning improvement initiatives with cultural norms.

In cultures that prioritize consensus, CIMM's implementation involves facilitating collaborative decision-making processes that involve a wide range of perspectives. In cultures with a top-down approach, CIMM's scalability ensures that improvement initiatives align with the decisions made at the top, while still allowing for localized adaptations.

Cultural attitudes toward innovation and risk-taking vary significantly. Some cultures embrace experimentation, while others favor stability. When scaling CIMM, understanding these cultural inclinations is crucial.

In innovative cultures, CIMM's adaptability involves encouraging and rewarding creative problem-solving and experimentation. In risk-averse cultures, CIMM's implementation involves emphasizing gradual, well-considered improvements that align with cultural comfort zones.

Effectively navigating cultural diversity when scaling CIMM requires strategic considerations. Equip teams with cultural sensitivity training to enhance their awareness and understanding of cultural differences and norms. Then, designate cultural liaisons within teams to bridge communication gaps, interpret cultural cues, and ensure that CIMM's principles are effectively communicated.

Tailor communication strategies and materials to resonate with the cultural preferences of different regions. Foster a culture of open feedback and collaboration, where employees from diverse cultural backgrounds feel comfortable sharing insights and concerns related to CIMM.

Navigating cultural diversity is an art that requires organizations to be attuned to the intricacies of their global workforce. Scaling the CIMM involves not just understanding cultural differences but embracing them. By recognizing that diverse cultural perspectives enrich the implementation process, CIMM's scalability becomes a conduit for a shared commitment to continuous improvement that transcends cultural boundaries. Through effective navigation of cultural diversity, organizations ensure that CIMM's transformative power resonates deeply with employees across the world, fostering a harmonized culture of improvement that is uniquely diverse and universally impactful.

Strategies for Successful Adaptation

As organizations scale the CIMM to diverse organizational structures and cultural contexts, employing thoughtful strategies for successful adaptation becomes crucial. These strategies ensure that CIMM's principles are not only embraced but also integrated seamlessly, fostering a culture of continuous improvement that resonates across the global organizational landscape.

Implementing cultural intelligence training equips teams with the knowledge and skills to navigate cultural differences effectively.

This training enhances their ability to interpret cultural cues, understand communication styles, and appreciate decision-making approaches. By fostering cultural sensitivity, teams are better prepared to adapt CIMM's principles in a way that aligns with local cultural norms.

Appointing cultural liaisons or ambassadors within teams can bridge communication gaps and facilitate effective adaptation. These individuals, with deep cultural understanding, serve as intermediaries, helping to interpret cultural nuances, ensuring accurate communication, and advocating for the successful implementation of CIMM within their cultural context.

Tailoring communication strategies and materials to resonate with the cultural preferences of different regions enhances understanding and engagement. This may involve using localized language, incorporating cultural references, and adapting communication styles to align with cultural norms. Customized communication ensures that CIMM's principles are effectively communicated and understood.

Establishing feedback loops and collaboration platforms that encourage open dialogue is essential for successful adaptation. Creating spaces where employees from diverse cultural backgrounds can share insights, provide feedback, and engage in discussions about CIMM's implementation enables organizations to capture diverse perspectives and adapt strategies accordingly.

Design CIMM as a flexible framework that accommodates localized adaptations. This involves preserving the core principles of CIMM while allowing for variations that align with cultural norms and organizational structures. The framework should provide guidance rather than rigid instructions, enabling teams to apply CIMM's principles in a manner that best suits their context.

Periodic assessments are essential to gauge the effectiveness of CIMM's adaptation. Organizations should establish mechanisms to evaluate how well CIMM's principles align with diverse contexts. Regular assessments allow for adjustments to be made based on feedback and insights, ensuring that CIMM's implementation remains relevant and impactful.

Encouraging cross-cultural learning within the organization enriches the adaptation process. Creating opportunities for employees to share experiences, best practices, and challenges across different regions fosters a sense of global community. This cross-cultural learning reinforces the idea that successful adaptation benefits from collective insights.

Leadership buy-in is instrumental in driving successful adaptation. When leaders actively support and participate in the adaptation process, it sends a strong message about the organization's commitment to embracing cultural diversity and fostering a global culture of continuous improvement.

Successful adaptation of the CIMM to diverse organizational structures and cultural contexts demands strategic forethought and a commitment to understanding and embracing differences. By employing these strategies, organizations can navigate the challenges of cultural diversity while harnessing the transformative power of CIMM's principles. Ultimately, the success of CIMM's adaptation lies in its ability to create a unified narrative of continuous improvement that resonates with employees across the globe, fostering a collaborative spirit that transcends geographical boundaries.

The adaptability of the CIMM to different organizational structures and cultures is a testament to its universality and effectiveness. By recognizing and embracing the diversity of structures and cultures, CIMM ensures that the pursuit of continuous improvement is inclusive and resonant across the global organizational landscape. This adaptability is not only a reflection of CIMM's dynamic nature but also a testament to its transformative power in promoting positive change on a global scale.

IMPLEMENTING CIMM IN DIVERSE SETTINGS—TAILORING FOR SUCCESS

The implementation of the CIMM across diverse settings brings to light the need for nuanced approaches that recognize the unique dynamics of each business environment. As organizations scale CIMM globally, the challenge lies not only in understanding the local intricacies but also in tailoring the framework to suit various contexts while preserving its overarching principles.

Recognizing Diverse Business Environments

The landscape of business environments is a rich tapestry woven with diverse threads of industries, market dynamics, and competitive scenarios. Implementing the CIMM demands a keen understanding of these diverse business contexts, acknowledging their nuances, challenges, and opportunities. CIMM's adaptability lies in recognizing and respecting the unique attributes of these environments.

Industries differ widely in terms of their processes, priorities, and customer expectations. Implementing CIMM requires tailoring strategies that align with industry-specific requirements. In manufacturing, CIMM's implementation might focus on lean principles, process optimization, and minimizing waste. The goal is to enhance efficiency and reduce production costs. Service-oriented sectors prioritize the customer experience. CIMM's application here might emphasize streamlined customer interactions, quick issue resolution, and personalized services.

The implementation of the CIMM is significantly influenced by the growth stage and maturity of the market in which an organization operates. Different market dynamics demand tailored approaches to CIMM's application, ensuring that improvement initiatives align with the unique challenges and opportunities presented by varying stages of market development.

In emerging markets, characterized by rapid economic expansion and changing consumer behaviors, CIMM's implementation focuses on navigating growth and capturing market share. CIMM strategies in emerging markets might emphasize agility and rapid adaptation to changing consumer preferences and market trends. Implementing CIMM here could involve scaling up operational infrastructure and distribution networks to accommodate growing demand. CIMM's application might include innovation strategies tailored to meet the specific needs of the emerging market's customer base.

In growing markets, where competition intensifies and market dynamics stabilize, CIMM's focus shifts to sustaining momentum and optimizing processes. CIMM's implementation could emphasize strategies for retaining customers, building brand loyalty, and maintaining a competitive edge. Implementing CIMM might involve streamlining processes, reducing operational inefficiencies, and enhancing the customer experience. CIMM's application might include initiatives to penetrate untapped segments within the growing market and expand the customer base.

In mature markets, where competition is fierce and market growth stabilizes, CIMM's implementation aims to enhance competitiveness and innovation. CIMM strategies in mature markets might focus on differentiation, developing unique value propositions, and standing out from competitors. Implementing CIMM could involve fostering a culture of continuous innovation to stay ahead in a saturated market. CIMM's application might emphasize fine-tuning operational processes, reducing costs, and optimizing resource utilization.

The implementation of the CIMM is intricately intertwined with the competitive landscape of the industry in which an organization operates. The dynamics of competition—ranging from intense rivalry to niche specialization—dictate how CIMM's principles are applied to foster excellence and maintain a competitive edge.

In industries characterized by intense competition, CIMM's implementation revolves around agility and innovation. CIMM strategies focus on swift adaptation to changing market conditions and customer preferences, enabling the organization to respond promptly to shifts. Implementing CIMM involves creating differentiators that set the organization apart from rivals. This might include unique product features, exceptional customer service, or innovative processes. CIMM's application could emphasize a deep understanding of customer needs and preferences, driving the development of tailored solutions.

In niche markets, where organizations cater to a specific segment with specialized needs, CIMM's focus is on achieving specialized excellence. CIMM's implementation involves honing expertise in the niche area to deliver solutions that precisely meet the demands of the target audience. Implementing CIMM here includes innovating within the niche's boundaries to enhance offerings and maintain relevance. CIMM's application could involve tailoring products, services, and processes to cater to the unique requirements of the niche market.

In regulated industries where adherence to standards is critical, CIMM's implementation centers around compliance and optimization. CIMM strategies ensure that compliance with regulatory standards is seamlessly integrated into the organization's improvement initiatives. Implementing CIMM involves optimizing processes to ensure efficiency while prioritizing safety, quality, and adherence to regulations. CIMM's application might include strategies to mitigate risks associated with non-compliance, ensuring the organization operates within legal boundaries.

Tailoring CIMM for Success

The versatility of the CIMM lies not only in its ability to scale across diverse settings but also in its capacity to be tailored for success within each unique context. As organizations embark on the journey of CIMM implementation, the art of tailoring the model to fit specific business environments becomes a critical determinant of its effectiveness and impact.

The foundational pillar of tailoring CIMM for success rests on designing the framework with inherent flexibility. While CIMM's core principles remain unwavering, creating a modular and adaptable structure allows for customization without compromising its integrity. This flexibility empowers organizations to navigate the intricate nuances of different business environments while still adhering to the overarching principles of continuous improvement.

Successful CIMM implementation demands the alignment of metrics and objectives with the unique goals and challenges of each business environment. Tailoring CIMM involves defining key performance indicators that resonate with the specific context. For example, in a customer-centric industry, metrics might focus on customer satisfaction and retention, while in a cost-sensitive sector, efficiency and waste reduction could be the primary metrics.

Adapting CIMM for success requires an acute awareness of the cultural norms within the business environment. Tailoring CIMM involves aligning improvement initiatives with these cultural norms to ensure that they are embraced and integrated seamlessly. This alignment enhances employee buy-in and participation, as CIMM's principles are contextualized to resonate with the values and beliefs of the workforce.

In an era of rapid technological advancement, successful CIMM implementation involves integrating technology that suits the local business environment. This might include the use of data analytics tools, process automation software, or communication platforms that align with the technological infrastructure of the organization. Integrating technology enhances the model's effectiveness and ensures efficient implementation.

Adaptation extends to training programs and support mechanisms. Tailoring CIMM for success involves designing training materials, workshops, and resources that address the specific challenges and learning styles within the business environment. This localized approach enhances understanding, engagement, and the practical application of CIMM's principles.

A pivotal aspect of tailoring CIMM for success involves instituting a feedback loop that captures insights from the implementation process. Regular assessments and feedback mechanisms allow organizations to course-correct, refine strategies, and optimize the model based on practical experiences and real-world challenges.

Real-world application of the CIMM is best illustrated through case-specific examples, where the principles of CIMM are tailored to suit distinct business environments. These examples provide insights into how CIMM's adaptable framework can be strategically customized to address unique challenges and opportunities within diverse settings.

In the healthcare industry, where patient safety and quality of care are paramount, CIMM's implementation might emphasize patient-centric improvement initiatives. Key metrics could include reduction in medical errors, improved patient outcomes, and enhanced patient satisfaction scores.

CIMM principles might be tailored to align with a culture of patient-centered care, involving both medical staff and administrative personnel in the improvement process. Training programs could focus on communication skills for healthcare professionals to enhance patient interactions and ensure a clear understanding of treatment plans.

In the technology sector, characterized by fast-paced innovation, CIMM's application might be geared toward fostering continuous innovation. Metrics could include the number of successful product releases, the speed of feature development, and the rate of adopting new technologies.

CIMM's principles could be adapted to encourage cross-functional collaboration, breaking down silos, and enhancing knowledge sharing. The implementation of CIMM could be aligned with agile methodologies, promoting iterative development cycles and rapid prototyping.

In the manufacturing industry, where process efficiency is crucial, CIMM could be tailored to optimize manufacturing processes. Metrics might include reducing production cycle times, minimizing defects, and optimizing resource utilization.

CIMM's implementation could align with lean manufacturing principles, focusing on waste reduction and streamlining production flows. The framework might emphasize employee involvement in identifying process bottlenecks and proposing improvement ideas.

For the retail sector, where customer experience drives success, CIMM's implementation could be customer-centric. Metrics could include net promoter score (NPS), customer feedback ratings, and repeat purchase rates.

CIMM might encourage frontline employees to contribute improvement ideas based on their interactions with customers. Tailoring CIMM could involve strategies to personalize customer interactions and enhance the overall shopping experience.

Recognizing the diversity of business environments is central to the successful implementation of the CIMM. By acknowledging the unique attributes of industries, market stages, and competitive scenarios, organizations can tailor CIMM strategies to suit specific contexts. Through this recognition and adaptation, CIMM becomes a dynamic tool that transcends generic approaches, fostering a culture of continuous improvement that resonates powerfully within the diverse landscape of business environments.

The art of tailoring the CIMM for success requires a delicate balance between customization and adherence to core principles. By embracing flexibility, aligning with cultural norms, and adapting strategies to suit local metrics, objectives, and challenges, organizations ensure that CIMM becomes a potent catalyst for positive change within each unique business environment. Through this tailored approach, CIMM transcends being a generic framework, evolving into a dynamic tool that fosters meaningful and sustainable continuous improvement across the diverse landscape of business contexts.

APPLYING CIMM GLOBALLY: CULTIVATING CROSS-CULTURAL CONTINUOUS IMPROVEMENT

The global landscape of business demands a unique set of tools and strategies to foster continuous improvement across borders and cultures. The CIMM emerges as a transformative framework that, when strategically applied, has the power to transcend cultural divides and instill a unified commitment to excellence. Through a combination of practical recommendations and illuminating case studies, professionals are equipped with the insights needed to navigate the complexities of global implementation and catalyze cross-cultural change.

Cultural Intelligence—A Foundation for Success

Implementing the CIMM on a global scale demands a profound understanding of cultural diversity and a high level of cultural intelligence. Cultural intelligence serves as the cornerstone for successful CIMM implementation, enabling professionals to navigate the intricate nuances of different cultural contexts while fostering a unified commitment to continuous improvement.

Cultural intelligence, often referred to as CQ, encompasses the capability to function effectively across diverse cultural settings. It involves not only recognizing cultural differences but also adapting behaviors, communication styles, and decision-making approaches to align with the cultural norms of each context. Cultural intelligence goes beyond surface-level understanding, delving into the underlying values, beliefs, and perspectives that shape behaviors.

Cultural intelligence begins with cultural sensitivity and awareness. Professionals embarking on global CIMM implementation must invest time and effort in learning about the cultures within which they operate. This involves studying cultural norms, communication patterns, business etiquette, and social dynamics. A profound respect for cultural diversity lays the groundwork for building authentic relationships and fostering trust.

Effective communication is at the heart of cultural intelligence. Professionals must be adept at adapting their communication styles to suit different cultural preferences. This might involve adjusting the level of formality, directness, or indirectness in communication. Cultural intelligence enables individuals to convey their messages clearly while respecting the cultural nuances of their audience.

Cultural intelligence encourages professionals to embrace diverse perspectives. Instead of assuming that a single approach fits all contexts, individuals with cultural intelligence actively seek to understand and appreciate varying viewpoints. This openness to different ways of thinking enriches problem-solving, decision-making, and innovation within the context of CIMM implementation.

Cultural intelligence is instrumental in building trust and relationships across cultural boundaries. It involves demonstrating genuine interest in others' cultures, acknowledging differences, and displaying a willingness to learn. This foundation of trust facilitates collaboration, encourages knowledge sharing, and paves the way for successful CIMM adoption within diverse teams.

Unilever, a consumer goods company, introduced the "U-Curve" model as part of its approach to cultural intelligence. This model emphasizes moving from the stages of "Denial" and "Defense" (where cultural differences are ignored or resisted) to "Minimization" and "Acceptance" (where differences are acknowledged). Ultimately, the goal is to reach the stages of "Adaptation" and "Integration," where cultural intelligence is fully embraced and integrated into daily practices. Unilever's case demonstrates how cultural intelligence can transform a global organization's approach to cross-cultural collaboration and CIMM implementation.

Cultural intelligence serves as the bedrock for successful CIMM implementation on a global scale. By nurturing cultural sensitivity, adaptable communication, and a genuine embrace of diverse perspectives, professionals are equipped to navigate the complexities of cultural diversity. This foundation enables CIMM strategies to resonate authentically with employees across borders and cultures, fostering a unified commitment to continuous improvement that enriches organizations on a global journey toward excellence.

Case Study of McDonald's Corporation: Streamlining Processes Worldwide

McDonald's Corporation, a global fast-food giant, has demonstrated remarkable success in implementing continuous improvement practices across its vast network of restaurants worldwide. Through a strategic focus on streamlining processes, enhancing efficiency, and maintaining consistent quality, McDonald's has established itself as a pioneer in applying the principles of continuous improvement on a global scale.

McDonald's recognized early on that global success requires more than a one-size-fits-all approach. Rather than imposing a uniform menu and operational model, the company embraced the concept of "glocalization." This approach involves tailoring offerings to local tastes and preferences while maintaining standardized processes that ensure quality and efficiency.

Drawing inspiration from lean manufacturing principles, McDonald's embraced the importance of minimizing waste and optimizing processes. This approach extended beyond individual restaurants to encompass the entire supply chain. By streamlining the flow of ingredients, optimizing cooking processes, and minimizing waiting times, McDonald's achieved efficiency gains that resonated across its global network.

While accommodating local preferences, McDonald's also sought to harmonize the customer experience. By implementing standardized customer service protocols worldwide, the company ensured a consistent level of service quality regardless of location. This balance between localization and standardization is at the heart of McDonald's continuous improvement journey.

McDonald's established global learning networks to facilitate knowledge sharing and best practice dissemination. These networks provided a platform for franchisees, managers, and employees from diverse regions to collaborate, exchange insights, and collectively identify opportunities for improvement. The cross-cultural exchange of ideas became a catalyst for innovation and efficiency enhancement.

McDonald's continuous improvement efforts yielded impressive outcomes. By optimizing processes, McDonald's reduced waiting times and enhanced operational efficiency, leading to increased customer satisfaction. Standardized processes ensured that the quality of food and service remained consistent across the globe, bolstering the brand's reputation.

The glocalization approach allowed McDonald's to cater to local tastes while maintaining a global brand identity. The global learning networks fostered an innovation culture where ideas flowed freely, contributing to the company's ongoing success.

McDonald's Corporation's success in streamlining processes worldwide demonstrates the transformative potential of continuous improvement practices on a global scale. By striking a balance between standardization and localization, embracing lean principles, and fostering collaboration across cultural boundaries, McDonald's has created a blueprint for how organizations can effectively implement continuous improvement strategies that resonate globally. This case study serves as an inspiration for organizations seeking to cultivate cross-cultural excellence through the principles of continuous improvement.

Case Study of BASF SE—Leveraging Global Network for Innovation

BASF SE, a leading chemical company, serves as an exemplary case of how to effectively implement continuous improvement practices on a global scale. By leveraging its extensive global network of subsidiaries, research centers, and operations, BASF has successfully fostered innovation, collaboration, and continuous improvement within a diverse array of cultural contexts.

At the core of BASF's success lies a strong commitment to nurturing an innovation-driven culture. The company emphasizes the importance of fostering an environment where employees are encouraged to contribute ideas and insights, regardless of their geographic location. This approach not only empowers individuals but also taps into the diverse expertise found within different cultural contexts.

BASF strategically established a comprehensive global network of research and development (R&D) centers. This network serves as a hub for sharing knowledge, expertise, and best practices across different locations.

By pooling resources and talents from diverse regions, BASF effectively harnesses the collective brainpower of its global workforce.

BASF's continuous improvement journey thrives on cross-cultural collaboration. The company recognizes that unique perspectives and approaches emerge from various cultural backgrounds. To capture these insights, BASF encourages collaboration across cultural boundaries, fostering a rich exchange of ideas that fuel innovation and process enhancement.

BASF's commitment to sustainability aligns with its global approach to continuous improvement. The company's focus on sustainability extends to all levels of its operations, from product development to supply chain management. By integrating sustainable practices across diverse cultural contexts, BASF creates a cohesive strategy that resonates globally.

BASF's approach to leveraging its global network for innovation has yielded significant outcomes. The company's emphasis on cross-cultural collaboration and idea-sharing has led to innovative breakthroughs in products, processes, and technologies.

The global R&D network facilitates efficient sharing of expertise, enabling teams to learn from each other's successes and challenges. BASF's commitment to sustainability aligns with diverse regulatory environments and customer demands, resulting in impactful solutions. BASF embraces cultural diversity as a strength, leveraging it to drive innovation and excellence across its global operations.

BASF SE's success story illustrates how an organization can effectively implement continuous improvement practices on a global scale by harnessing the power of its global network. By nurturing an innovation culture, establishing a robust R&D network, promoting cross-cultural collaboration, and prioritizing sustainability, BASF has created a blueprint for organizations aspiring to achieve cross-cultural excellence through continuous improvement strategies. This case study underscores the transformative potential of embracing cultural diversity as an asset and leveraging it to drive innovation and success across the global business landscape.

The journey to apply CIMM on a global scale is a testament to the unifying power of continuous improvement. By embracing cultural intelligence, tailoring strategies, and drawing inspiration from successful case studies, professionals can foster a culture of excellence that transcends borders and cultures. CIMM becomes more than a model; it becomes a conduit for a shared commitment to growth, innovation, and sustainable success that resonates harmoniously with diverse voices across the global business landscape. Through these tools and strategies, the vision of cross-cultural continuous improvement transforms into a tangible reality that enriches organizations worldwide.

FROM TRADITIONAL LEAN TO CIMM: A PARADIGM SHIFT IN CONTINUOUS IMPROVEMENT

The evolution of continuous improvement methodologies has been marked by a transformative journey from traditional lean approaches to the innovative paradigm of the CIMM. This journey reflects the changing demands of modern business environments, and the CIMM approach emerges as a dynamic response that addresses the limitations of traditional methods while harnessing their core principles for a new era of excellence.

Traditional Lean Methodologies—The Foundation

Traditional lean methodologies have served as the cornerstone of continuous improvement practices for decades. Rooted in the Toyota Production System (TPS) philosophy, these methodologies have revolutionized industries by focusing on waste reduction, process optimization, and the pursuit of operational excellence. Understanding the key principles and concepts of traditional lean methodologies is essential to appreciating their role as the foundation upon which the innovative approach of the CIMM is built.

Traditional lean methodologies prioritize the identification and elimination of different forms of waste, including overproduction, waiting times, unnecessary transportation, excessive inventory, defects, and underutilized talent. The goal is to optimize processes and minimize non-value-added activities.

The principle of Kaizen underscores the importance of small, incremental improvements that involve every employee. It promotes a culture of constant learning, experimentation, and refinement to enhance efficiency and effectiveness.

Just In Time (JIT) emphasizes producing and delivering products or services only when they are needed, thereby reducing excess inventory and associated costs. This principle requires synchronizing production with customer demand to minimize waste and lead times.

An integral part of traditional lean methodologies is a deep respect for the knowledge, skills, and contributions of employees. Empowering employees to identify and solve problems enhances their engagement and drives continuous improvement.

The 5S methodology (Sort, Set in order, Shine, Standardize, Sustain) focuses on organizing and maintaining the workplace for optimal efficiency and safety. A clean, well-organized environment contributes to better productivity and employee morale.

Traditional lean methodologies laid the groundwork for a culture of continuous improvement in organizations. They transformed manufacturing and operational processes, driving improvements in quality, cost reduction, and lead time reduction. However, as business environments become more complex, global, and customer-focused, traditional lean approaches encountered limitations in addressing broader strategic and cultural aspects of improvement.

The transformative journey from traditional lean to CIMM recognizes the strengths of traditional methodologies while integrating new dimensions to address modern challenges. CIMM extends the focus beyond operational processes, encompassing cultural transformation, strategic alignment, and cross-cultural considerations. By building upon the foundation of traditional lean, CIMM offers a comprehensive and adaptable framework for achieving excellence in a rapidly evolving world.

Traditional lean methodologies have played a pivotal role in shaping the continuous improvement landscape. These foundational principles have paved the way for innovation and transformation, acknowledging that as businesses evolve, their improvement strategies must evolve as well. By understanding the essence of traditional lean methodologies, organizations are better equipped to appreciate the journey that led to the development of the CIMM, which builds upon these principles while embracing the demands of modern business dynamics.

Limitations of Traditional Lean—Navigating Constraints

While traditional lean methodologies have been instrumental in driving continuous improvement in various industries, they are not without limitations. As business environments become more complex and dynamic, these limitations have become increasingly apparent. Recognizing and addressing these constraints has paved the way for the evolution toward the innovative CIMM.

One of the key limitations of traditional lean methodologies is their narrow focus on operational processes. While optimizing processes is critical, this approach often neglects broader strategic considerations, such as alignment with organizational goals, market dynamics, and innovation. This limitation can hinder the organization's ability to adapt to changing customer needs and competitive landscapes.

Traditional lean methodologies can sometimes be applied rigidly, leading to a "one-size-fits-all" approach. This rigidity can be counterproductive when organizations operate in diverse cultural and market contexts. The lack of flexibility to tailor methodologies to suit specific challenges and opportunities can result in suboptimal outcomes and missed opportunities for improvement.

In today's rapidly evolving business landscape, organizations must be agile and innovative to remain competitive. Traditional lean methodologies may struggle to keep up with the demands of innovation, customer-centricity, and digital transformation. Their focus on process optimization might not fully address the need for creative problem-solving, adaptability, and the ability to embrace new technologies.

While traditional lean methodologies emphasize process improvement, they may not comprehensively address cultural transformation. Organizations that want to drive sustainable change must also consider fostering a culture of continuous improvement, empowering employees to drive innovation, and aligning the organization's values with its improvement goals.

Traditional lean methodologies can sometimes lack direct alignment with an organization's strategic objectives. Improving processes in isolation, without considering how these improvements contribute to broader goals, may lead to suboptimal resource allocation and misaligned efforts.

The limitations of traditional lean methodologies have spurred the evolution toward the CIMM. By acknowledging and addressing these limitations, organizations are better equipped to adapt, innovate, and drive sustainable improvement in a rapidly changing business landscape. CIMM's innovative approach builds upon the strengths of traditional lean while embracing the multifaceted demands of modern business, ensuring that continuous improvement remains a strategic cornerstone for success.

Enter CIMM—A New Approach to Continuous Improvement

The evolution of continuous improvement methodologies has brought forth the groundbreaking concept of the CIMM. CIMM represents a new paradigm in the realm of continuous improvement, synthesizing the core principles of traditional lean methodologies with innovative strategies to create a holistic framework that addresses the complexities of modern business environments.

CIMM builds on the foundation of traditional lean methodologies while recognizing their limitations. It takes a comprehensive approach that goes beyond the narrow focus on operational processes and embraces multiple dimensions of organizational excellence.

CIMM recognizes that achieving sustainable improvement requires a cultural shift. Organizations must cultivate a culture of continuous improvement, innovation, and collaboration. This cultural transformation involves empowering employees, fostering a growth mindset, and nurturing an environment where experimentation is encouraged.

It emphasizes the importance of aligning continuous improvement efforts with an organization's overarching strategic goals. Improvement initiatives are not seen in isolation but as integral components of achieving the organization's vision and mission.

CIMM places a strong emphasis on understanding and meeting customer needs. Improvement efforts are directed toward creating value for customers, enhancing their experience, and ensuring that processes are designed to deliver exceptional products or services.

A key advantage of CIMM lies in its scalability and flexibility. Unlike traditional lean methodologies that may struggle to adapt to diverse organizational structures and cultural contexts, CIMM offers a modular framework that can be tailored to suit the specific needs and challenges of different environments. Organizations can implement CIMM at their own pace and adjust strategies as they progress through different levels of maturity.

This model integrates various elements of continuous improvement, including lean principles, Six Sigma methodologies, change management strategies, and cultural transformation approaches. This integration creates a cohesive framework that enables organizations to address a wide range of improvement objectives while fostering synergy among various initiatives.

Recognizing the global nature of business today, CIMM also addresses the importance of cultural intelligence. It provides strategies for navigating cross-cultural challenges and leveraging cultural diversity as an asset. CIMM acknowledges that a one-size-fits-all approach is not effective in a world characterized by diverse organizational cultures and global market dynamics.

The CIMM signifies an evolutionary leap in the realm of continuous improvement. By expanding beyond the traditional lean methodologies, CIMM offers organizations an innovative framework that integrates cultural transformation, strategic alignment, customer-centricity, and flexibility. This comprehensive approach equips organizations to thrive in the dynamic, customer-driven, and culturally diverse landscape of the modern business world. Through CIMM, organizations embark on a transformative journey that propels them toward sustainable excellence, adaptive growth, and continuous innovation.

The transformative journey from traditional lean methodologies to the innovative approach of the CIMM reflects the dynamic nature of business and the need for adaptive and comprehensive continuous improvement strategies. While traditional lean methods remain foundational, CIMM emerges as a response to the challenges of a globalized, customer-centric, and rapidly changing business landscape. By embracing the principles of CIMM, organizations position themselves to navigate complexity, achieve sustainable excellence, and embark on a continuous improvement journey that is tailored to the demands of the modern world.

CULTURAL SHIFT, CHANGE MANAGEMENT, AND ADAPTIVE LEADERSHIP: PILLARS OF SUSTAINABLE CONTINUOUS IMPROVEMENT

The journey from traditional lean methodologies to the innovative approach of the CIMM underscores the pivotal role of a cultural shift, effective change management, and adaptive leadership. These pillars serve as the bedrock upon which the transformation toward sustainable continuous improvement is built, ensuring that strategies resonate, initiatives are embraced, and excellence becomes ingrained in the organizational DNA.

Cultural Shift—Nurturing the Foundation

A profound and lasting transformation in the realm of continuous improvement begins with a cultural shift. This shift is not merely a change in practices or processes; it's a fundamental change in the way an organization thinks, operates, and perceives its journey toward excellence.

Nurturing a culture that embraces continuous improvement as a core value lays the foundation for sustained success and innovation.

At the heart of a cultural shift is the cultivation of a growth mindset. This mindset values learning, adaptation, and embracing challenges as opportunities for growth. When employees across all levels of an organization adopt a growth mindset, they are more likely to actively seek ways to improve processes, generate innovative ideas, and collaborate effectively.

A cultural shift empowers employees to become drivers of change. Instead of relying solely on top-down directives, employees are encouraged to voice their suggestions, experiment with new approaches, and take ownership of their work. This empowerment taps into the wealth of knowledge and creativity within the workforce, leading to more efficient processes, improved products, and enhanced customer experiences.

A culture of continuous improvement thrives on open communication and collaboration. When employees are encouraged to share their insights and work together to solve problems, the result is a more holistic and effective approach to improvement. Silos are broken down, and cross-functional teams can address challenges from multiple perspectives, leading to comprehensive solutions.

Leaders play a pivotal role in shaping organizational culture. When leaders model a commitment to continuous improvement, it sends a powerful message that this mindset is not optional but an integral part of how the organization operates. Leaders who are open to feedback, willing to learn, and responsive to change set the tone for a culture where improvement is the norm.

A cultural shift toward continuous improvement essentially transforms the organization into a learning organization. Learning becomes embedded in the fabric of daily work, and mistakes are seen as opportunities for improvement rather than as failures. This mindset shift not only enhances employee engagement but also accelerates innovation as the organization becomes adept at adapting to new challenges.

Nurturing a cultural shift requires continuous effort. It involves ongoing communication, reinforcement of core values, and recognition of employees who embody the improvement mindset. Celebrating successes, sharing stories of positive change, and acknowledging the efforts of those who champion improvement initiatives help sustain the cultural shift over time.

In the journey toward sustainable continuous improvement, a cultural shift is the catalyst that drives transformation. This shift ignites a passion for learning, innovation, and collaboration that permeates the organization's ethos. By nurturing a culture that embraces growth mindsets, empowers employees, fosters collaboration, and values adaptation, organizations create an environment where continuous improvement becomes not just a goal but a way of life. This foundation sets the stage for embracing the principles of effective change management and adaptive leadership, ultimately propelling the organization toward enduring excellence in a dynamic business landscape.

Change Management—Guiding the Transformation

In the journey from traditional lean methodologies to the innovative CIMM, effective change management emerges as a linchpin that guides the transformation process. Change management is the strategic and structured approach organizations use to navigate the complexities of change, ensuring that transitions are smooth, employees are engaged, and improvement initiatives are successfully integrated into the organizational fabric.

Change is inherent in any improvement initiative, but it can also evoke resistance, uncertainty, and disruption. Effective change management involves understanding the dynamics of change—why people resist it, how it affects different aspects of the organization, and what strategies can mitigate negative reactions. This understanding allows organizations to proactively address challenges and create a supportive environment for change.

Communication is paramount in change management. Clear, consistent, and transparent communication helps employees understand the reasons for change, the benefits it brings, and how their roles might evolve. Open channels of communication also provide an opportunity for employees to voice concerns, ask questions, and seek clarification, fostering a sense of involvement and ownership in the process.

Effective change management engages stakeholders at all levels of the organization. From leadership to front line employees, involving stakeholders in the planning and decision-making process builds buy-in and a sense of shared ownership. This involvement not only enhances the quality of decisions but also creates a sense of responsibility for the success of the change initiative.

Change management ensures that employees have the necessary resources, tools, and support to navigate the changes successfully. This might involve providing training, offering coaching, and creating forums for sharing best practices. When employees feel adequately supported, they are more likely to embrace the changes and integrate new practices into their daily routines.

Resistance to change is natural, but it can hinder progress. Effective change management involves identifying sources of resistance and developing strategies to address them. Whether it's addressing concerns, debunking myths, or highlighting the positive aspects of change, proactive measures can help overcome resistance and create a more receptive environment.

Change management is not a one-time event; it's an ongoing process. Effective change management involves monitoring the progress of change initiatives, gathering feedback, and adapting strategies as needed. This flexibility ensures that the change process remains aligned with organizational goals and responds to emerging challenges or opportunities.

Change management serves as the bridge that connects improvement strategies to their successful implementation. By understanding the dynamics of change, communicating effectively, engaging stakeholders, providing support, managing resistance, and adapting strategies, organizations ensure that the transformation journey is guided by a clear roadmap. When change management is effectively executed, it instills confidence, minimizes disruptions, and empowers employees to embrace the journey toward continuous improvement. Through change management, organizations navigate the complexities of transformation with intention, foresight, and a focus on sustained success.

Adaptive Leadership—Guiding Transformational Change

In the evolution from traditional lean methodologies to the innovative CIMM, the role of adaptive leadership emerges as a crucial factor in guiding transformational change. Adaptive leadership represents a dynamic and responsive approach to leading change, one that is well suited to the complexities and uncertainties of the modern business landscape.

Adaptive leadership recognizes that today's business environment is characterized by rapid change, uncertainty, and ambiguity. It acknowledges that traditional leadership models may not suffice in situations where answers aren't readily available, and challenges require creative problem-solving. Adaptive leaders are comfortable operating in the gray areas, where solutions need to be co-created and strategies adjusted based on emerging information.

Central to adaptive leadership is flexibility and resilience. These leaders are willing to pivot, adjust, and even discard strategies that no longer serve the evolving needs of the organization. They embrace change as an opportunity for growth, and their willingness to learn from failures and setbacks sets the tone for the organization's approach to improvement.

Adaptive leaders empower their teams by fostering an environment of experimentation and learning. They encourage teams to explore new ideas, test hypotheses, and take calculated risks. By doing so, they create a safe space for innovation, allowing employees to contribute their insights and contribute to the continuous improvement journey.

Adaptive leaders' model and encourage a growth mindset—a belief that challenges are opportunities to learn and improve. They inspire their teams to see setbacks as stepping stones to success and to view change as a chance to develop new skills. This mindset not only enhances resilience but also drives a culture of continuous learning and improvement.

Adaptive leadership is collaborative and inclusive. These leaders recognize that diverse perspectives lead to richer solutions. They actively seek input from employees at all levels, encouraging cross-functional collaboration and valuing contributions from diverse backgrounds. This approach fosters a sense of ownership and shared responsibility for the organization's transformational journey.

Adaptive leaders lead by example, demonstrating the behaviors and attitudes they expect from their teams. They show that they are open to feedback, willing to embrace change, and dedicated to continuous improvement. This authenticity and transparency inspire confidence in the organization's direction and encourage employees to adopt similar mindsets.

In the transition from traditional lean methodologies to the CIMM, adaptive leadership emerges as the guiding force that navigates transformational change. By embracing uncertainty, practicing flexibility, empowering teams, and cultivating a growth mindset, adaptive leaders create an environment where change is embraced rather than feared. Through their collaborative approach and willingness to adapt, they inspire their teams to be agile, innovative, and resilient—qualities that are essential in driving sustainable continuous improvement in the ever-evolving business landscape. Adaptive leadership not only steers the transformational journey but also sets the stage for the integration of a cultural shift and effective change management, completing the trinity of pillars that propel organizations toward enduring excellence.

Synchronizing the Pillars for Success—A Holistic Approach to Excellence

In the transformational journey from traditional lean methodologies to the innovative CIMM, the synchronization of three essential pillars—a cultural shift, effective change management, and adaptive leadership—emerges as a holistic approach that drives sustainable success. When these pillars work in harmony, organizations create a powerful framework that empowers individuals, guides transformation, and cultivates a culture of excellence.

The cultural shift, effective change management, and adaptive leadership are not isolated entities; they are interdependent and complementary. Their strengths combine to create a synergy that propels the organization toward continuous improvement and sustainable excellence.

A cultural shift nurtures an environment where employees are motivated to embrace change, experiment with new ideas, and collaborate effectively. It sets the tone for the entire transformation journey, fostering a mindset that values improvement as an intrinsic part of organizational culture.

Change management provides the roadmap for navigating the transformation process. It ensures that employees are engaged, communication is clear, and resistance is managed effectively. By incorporating change management principles, organizations create a smoother transition and minimize disruptions.

Adaptive leaders guide the organization through uncertainty, making quick decisions based on emerging information, and adapting strategies as needed. Their dynamic approach aligns with the evolving nature of change, empowering employees to navigate challenges and seize opportunities.

Adaptive leadership serves as the glue that binds these pillars together. Adaptive leaders inspire the cultural shift by modeling the desired behavior and mindset. They communicate change effectively, engage stakeholders, and provide the support needed to implement new strategies. Their willingness to adapt ensures that the organization remains responsive to changing circumstances.

Synchronizing the pillars requires a shared vision and alignment across all levels of the organization. Leadership, employees, and stakeholders must collectively understand the purpose of the transformation, its benefits, and the role each individual plays in its success. This alignment fosters a sense of ownership, collaboration, and accountability, creating a united front that drives the organization forward.

When the cultural shift, effective change management, and adaptive leadership work in harmony, they create a virtuous cycle of improvement. A cultural shift that values learning and innovation fuels effective change management, leading to smoother transitions and increased employee engagement. Adaptive leadership guides the process, making adjustments based on feedback, and ensuring that the organization remains agile and responsive.

In the grand narrative of transforming from traditional lean methodologies to the CIMM, synchronizing the pillars of a cultural shift, effective change management, and adaptive leadership emerges as a blueprint for sustainable excellence. This holistic approach acknowledges that excellence isn't achieved through methodologies alone; it's the result of a dynamic interplay between culture, transformational guidance, and adaptive responsiveness. By embracing these pillars, organizations set the stage for a journey that transcends frameworks, embraces change, and paves the way for a future defined by continuous improvement, innovation, and enduring success.

In the transformative journey from traditional lean methodologies to the CIMM, the importance of a cultural shift, effective change management, and adaptive leadership cannot be overstated. These pillars collectively create a culture of excellence where improvement is not just a goal but a way of life. By embracing a culture that values learning, navigates change effectively, and is guided by adaptive leadership, organizations lay the foundation for sustainable continuous improvement that endures in the face of evolving business landscapes and challenges. Through these pillars, organizations transcend beyond methodologies and frameworks, embarking on a journey toward holistic transformation and a future of excellence.

In the intricate dance between tradition and innovation, I tried to guide through a labyrinth of profound insights into the dynamic world of organizational evolution in this chapter. As the final strokes are drawn, we emerge with a heightened understanding of the pivotal interplay between scalability and global considerations, interwoven with the fabric of the CIMM.

The journey embarked upon transcends the mere pursuit of operational efficiency. It underscores the strategic imperative of scalability, a concept that propels organizations beyond conventional confines. Scalability, as we have observed, is not confined to the mechanical expansion of processes; it signifies an organizational ethos that seamlessly adapts to varying structures, cultures, and markets. Within this dynamic construct resides CIMM, a paradigm-shifting framework that transcends conventional improvement methodologies, providing a blueprint for holistic excellence.

At the core of this exploration lies a profound realization—the transformational power of a cultural shift. This shift embodies a seismic change in the way organizations perceive improvement. It nurtures a fertile ground where innovation, collaboration, and continuous learning flourish. Through this lens, continuous improvement ceases to be a strategy confined to manuals; it metamorphoses into a pervasive ethos that permeates the very soul of the organization.

The discourse of effective change management adds depth to the narrative, illuminating the pragmatic complexities that accompany transformation. It underscores the art of navigating change with finesse—from communication to stakeholder engagement—ensuring a harmonious transition. Parallel to this is the emergence of adaptive leadership, a beacon of resilience and agility in the face of uncertainty. Adaptive leadership transcends the realm of convention, guiding organizations through uncharted waters, and embedding adaptability as a cornerstone of their identity.

As the crescendo of these elements reverberates, a symphony of holistic success emerges. Scalability, cultural shift, effective change management, and adaptive leadership converge to sculpt an ecosystem where innovation thrives, change is embraced, and resilience prevails. This holistic approach lays the groundwork for organizations to flourish amid dynamic challenges, fostering a culture of enduring excellence and unwavering adaptability.

In the concluding notes of this chapter, we stand at the precipice of transformation, armed with a profound understanding of the intricate dance between scalability and global considerations. The principles elucidated within these pages beckon organizations to embrace this transformative journey, navigating complexities, and fostering a future where the pursuit of excellence knows no bounds.

Bibliography

Al Saqi Books. (1984). The Crusades through Arab Eyes. Amin Maalouf. https://www.amazon.com/Crusades-through-Arab-Eyes/dp/0863560230

Amabile, T. M., & Kramer, S. J. (2011). The Progress Principle: Using Small Wins to Ignite Joy, Engagement, and Creativity at Work. http://progressprinciple.com/books/single/the-progress-principle

Ballé, M. (2019). Lead with Lean: On Lean Leadership and Practice. https://www.thriftbooks.com/w/lead-with-lean-on-lean-leadership-and-practice_michael-ball/13885971/

California Manufacturing Technology Consulting (CMTC). (n.d.). The Benefits of Adopting a Continuous Improvement Approach. https://www.cmtc.com/blog/the-benefits-of-adopting-a-continuous-improvement-approach

Davenport, T. H., Harris, J., & Shapiro, J. (2010). Competing on Talent Analytics. https://hbr.org/2010/10/competing-on-talent-analytics

Dweck, C. S. (2016). What Having a "Growth Mindset" Actually Means. https://hbr.org/2016/01/what-having-a-growth-mindset-actually-means

Eisenbeiss, S. A., Knippenberg, D. V., & Boerner, S. (2008). Transformational Leadership and Team Innovation: Integrating Team Climate Principles. https://www.researchgate.net/publication/23489233_Transformational_Leadership_and_Team_Innovation_Integrating_Team_Climate_Principles

Gallup. (n.d.). What Is Employee Engagement and How Do You Improve It?. https://www.gallup.com/workplace/285674/improve-employee-engagement-workplace.aspx

Henker, N., Sonnentag, S., & Unger, D. (2015). Transformational Leadership and Employee Creativity: The Mediating Role of Promotion Focus and Creative Process Engagement. *Journal of Business and Psychology*. https://link.spinger.com/article/10.1007/s10869-014-9348-7

Highsmith, J. (2023). *Adaptive Leadership: Accelerating Enterprise Agility*. Addison-Wesley Professional.

Hope, J. & Player S. (2012). *Beyond Performance Management: Why, When, and How to Use 40 Tools and Best Practices for Superior Business Performance*. Harvard Business Review Press

Human Systems Integration. (n.d.). What Is a Learning Ecosystem and How Does It Support Corporate Strategy? https://hsi.com/blog/what-is-a-learning-ecosystem-and-how-does-it-support-corporate-strategy

Kamel, S. H. (2022). *Leading Change in Challenging Times: Lessons of Disruption and Innovation from Egypt: Thoughts, Observations, and Reflections*. Independently Published.

Kotter, J. P. (1995). Leading Change: Why Transformation Efforts Fail. https://hbr.org/1995/05/leading-change-why-transformation-efforts-fail-2

Kotter, J. P. (2022). Leading Change in Challenging Times: Observations on the Change in Leadership Over the Years.

Kouzes, J. M., & Posner, B. Z. (2023). *The Leadership Challenge: How to Make Extraordinary Things Happen in Organizations*. John Wiley and Sons.

Kropsu-Vehkapera, H., & Isoherranen, V. (2018). Lean Approach in Knowledge Work. https://www.researchgate.net/publication/325228719_Lean_approach_in_knowledge_work

Liker, J. (2004). The Toyota Way: 14 Management Principles from the World's Greatest Manufacturer. https://vietnamwcm.files.wordpress.com/2008/07/mcgraw-hill-the toyotaway-14managementprinciples.pdf

Nawaiseh, K., Shibly, M., & Alawamleh, H. A. (2022). The Relationship between Administrative Empowerment and Continuous Improvement: An Empirical Study. https://www.researchgate.net/publication/353466660_The_Relationship_between_Administrative_Empowerment_and_Continuous_Improvement_An_Empirical_Study

Womack, J. P., & Jones, D. T. (2003). Lean Thinking: Banish Waste and Create Wealth in Your Corporation. https://www.amazon.com/Lean-Thinking-Corporation-Revised-Updated/dp/0743249275

Womack, J. P., Jones, D. T., & Roos, D. (1990). The Machine That Changed the World: The Story of Lean Production. https://www.amazon.ca/Machine-That-Changed-World-Revolutionizing/dp/0743299795/ref=asc_df_0743299795?tag=bingshopdesk-20&linkCode=df0&hvadid=79989562644725&hvnetw=o&hvqmt=e&hvbmt=be&hvdev=c&hvlocint=&hvlocphy=&hvtargid=pla-4583589107539387&psc=1

Index

A

Acme Manufacturing, 88–89
adaptability/adaptation of CIMM; *see also* scalability
  agile responses and, 75–76
  assessments, 116
  collaboration platforms, 116
  communication, 116
  cross-cultural learning, 116
  cultural diversity, 107, 114–115, 117
  cultural intelligence training, 115–116
  cultural liaisons or ambassadors, 116
  feedback loops, 116
  leadership buy-in, 117
  organizational structures, 112–114, 117
  strategies, 115–117
"Adapting Lean for Knowledge Work" (Cusumano and Nobeoka), 36
adaptive leadership; *see also* leadership
  cultural shift and, 136
  empowering teams, 135
  flexibility, 135
  growth mindset and, 135
  holistic approach, 136–138; *see also* change management; cultural shift/transformation
  resilience, 135, 138
  transformational change and, 134–136
Adaptive Leadership: Accelerating Enterprise Agility (Sahota), 41
adaptive planning, 40–41
"Advances in Business-Related Scientific Research Journal", 43
alignment of objectives, 36
Amabile, Teresa M., 41
Amazon
  cross-functional collaboration, 46
  customer-centric innovation, 87–88
  experimentation and innovation, 46
American Psychological Association, 44
Anderson, Michael, 36
anecdotal narratives, 93–97
  General Electric (GE), 95
  Microsoft, 94–95
  RetailCo, 93–94
  TechWave, 96–97
Apple, 48

B

Balle, Michael, 37
BASF SE, 125–127
"Beyond Performance Management: Why, When, and How to Use 40 Tools and Best Practices for Superior Business Performance", 43
Brewer, Mike, 12
Bridges, William, 61

C

capability advancement, 4
celebrating achievements/milestones, 31–32, 41, 44
centralized organizational structures, 113
change agents, 58, 74, 80–81
  adaptability, 75–76
  creating network of, 70–71
  frontline employees as, 76–78
change management, 21–22, 103
  challenges in, 74
  communication and, 133
  cross-functional teams, 70
  holistic approach, 136–138; *see also* adaptive leadership; cultural shift/transformation
  leadership and, 66, 71
  lean principles integrated with, 73–75, 80–82
  network of change agents, 70–71
  as an ongoing process, 134
  readiness assessment, 70

resistance to, 134
scaling CIMM, 107
stages, 70–71
stakeholders engagement, 133
step-by-step approach, 70
strategies/techniques, 61, 74
sustainable continuous improvement, 133–134
Chartier, Nicolas, 37
checklist approach, 30
collaboration, 19–20
collective consciousness, 63
commitment of leaders/leadership, 29–30, 38–39, 46, 62, 66, 68–69, 133
communication, 19–20, 30–31
change management and, 133
cultural diversity, 114
cultural intelligence (CQ), 123–124
cultural shift/transformation, 132
scaling CIMM, 107
communities of practice, 44
consistency, scaling CIMM and, 106–107
continuous improvement maturity model (CIMM), 17–19
adaptability, *see* adaptability/adaptation of CIMM
change management, *see* change management
cultural shift and, *see* cultural shift/transformation
diverse settings (tailoring for success), 117–122
embedding, 78–82
flexibility, *see* flexibility
foundations, 60–61
healthcare industry, 121
holistic approach to excellence, 136–138
innovative framework, 131
Lean Assimilation (Stage 2), 62–64
Lean Initiation (Stage 1), 61–62
Lean Mastery (Stage 3), 64–65
Lean Transformation (Stage 4), 65–67
manufacturing industry and, 121
measuring impact (quantifiable success stories), 97–101
retail sector and, 121
scaling/scalability, *see* scalability
sustainable improvement, 131–138
synergistic impact, 73–75
technology sector and, 121
traditional lean methodologies *vs.*, 129–131
understanding, 103–105
"Creating a Learning Organization" (Garvin), 40
cross-functional teams, 70, 75, 77, 90, 132
cultural assessment, 54
cultural change, 19–21
cultural diversity, 126, 130
adaptability/adaptation, 107, 114–115, 117
communication, 114
decision-making approaches, 114
respect for, 123
scaling CIMM, 107–108, 114–115
cultural intelligence (CQ), 122–124, 131
communication, 123–124
diverse perspectives, 123–124
sensitivity and awareness, 123–124
training, 115–116
trust and relationships, 123
"U-Curve" model, 123
cultural sensitivity, 107, 110, 115–116, 123–124
cultural shift/transformation, 37, 102
as a catalyst, 68
communication and collaboration, 132
core values and mission statement, 69
cross-functional collaboration, 69
empowering employees, 132
growth mindset and, 132
holistic approach, 136–138
innovation workshops, 69
leadership commitment, 68–69, 133
practical steps, 68
stages, 68–69
sustainable continuous improvement, 131–133
culture of continuous improvement, 45–50
aligning Lean principles with organization's identity, 31
creating, 73
empowering employees, 47
fostering, 63
infrastructure, 46–47
laying foundation for change, 45–46, 63–64

leadership commitment, 46
learning organization and, 46
measurement system, 48
sustainability and scalability, 48–49
technology and innovation, 47–48
transitioning to, 31, 42–45
Cuneo, Dennis, 10–11
customer satisfaction, 104
Cusumano, Michael A., 36

D

data
CIMM technique, 54
introspection, 54
perceptions and, 55–57
data collection and analysis, 78
data-driven culture, 48
data-driven decision-making, 56–59
Davis, Mark, 37
decentralized organizational structures, 113
design thinking, 48
Dweck, Carol, 43

E

Eisenhower, Dwight D., 41
embedding CIMM in organizational DNA, 78–82
communication, 80
consistent effort, 80
integration of lean with change management, 80–82
leaders, 79
onboarding and induction, 78–79
performance management, 78–79
recognition, 79
training and development programs, 80
employee
empowering, *see* empowerment (of employees/team)
engagement, 43
as influencers, 76–78
"Employee Engagement and Performance" (Gallup Organization), 39
"Empowerment and Continuous Improvement: An Empirical Study", 43
empowerment (of employees/team), 33–34, 39, 46, 69, 71, 73, 80–81; *see also* continuous improvement maturity model
change management and, 21
continuous improvement and, 35, 47
cultural change and, 20, 132
data/information as a tool of, 56, 58–59
decentralized structures and, 113
as influencers, 76–78
Kaizen and, 14–15
leaders and, 23, 64–66, 72, 135–136
traditional lean methodologies, 127–128
transitioning to culture of improvement, 43
E-Trade Emporium, 91–92

F

"Faster, Better, Cheaper" in the History of Manufacturing (Roser), 10
5S methodology, 128
flexibility, 41, 85, 107–109, 130, 134
adaptive leadership, 135
organizational structures, 113
tailoring CIMM, 120, 122
Ford, 13
data-driven decision-making, 47
Six Sigma implementation, 47
Foster, Rebecca, 39
"A Framework for Continuous Improvement in Higher Education", 40

G

Gallup Organization research, 39
gap (between Lean and continuous improvement)
factors increasing, 29–33
overview, 28–29
Garvin, David A., 40
General Electric (GE)
CIMM and, 84–85, 95
leadership commitment, 46
resurgence, 84–85
General Motors (GM), 8–12
global implications of scaling CIMM, 109–110

GlobalLogistics, 99–100
"Global Manufacturing System" (TPS), 12
glocalization, 124–125; *see also* McDonald's Corporation
Google's "20% Time" initiative, 48–49

H

healthcare industry, 121
holistic approach to excellence, 136–138
holistic view of value, 37–38
Holt, Philip, 15

I

improvements, 4–5
influence model, 2
informal learning networks, 44
infrastructure of continuous improvement, 46–47
innovation, 47–48; *see also* technology
"An Integrated Problem-Solving Framework for Continuous Improvement", 38
iteration and learning, 36

J

Japanese culture, 3
Japanese work ethic, 3
Jidoka, 13–14
Johnson, Emily, 35
Jones, Daniel, 36
The Journal of Applied Behavioral Science, 43
Journal of Continuous Improvement in Higher Education, 40
Journal of Lean Systems, 38
just-in-time (JIT), 13–15, 117

K

Kaizen, 14, 127
Kaizen Blitz, 17
Kammüller, Mathias, 8
key performance indicators (KPIs), 5, 48, 78, 120
Kotter, John, 37, 61
Kouzes, James M., 45

L

laws and regulations, 106–107; *see also* scalability
leadership, 4
  adaptive, *see* adaptive leadership
  attributes/qualities, 22–24, 64–66, 71–72
  autonomy, 72
  change agents and, 78
  commitment, 29–30, 38–39, 46, 62, 66, 68–69, 133
  as a cultural catalyst, 63
  culture and, 20, 29–30
  delegating responsibilities, 72
  improvement initiatives, 44
  Lean Assimilation (Stage 2) and, 63
  Lean Initiation (Stage 1) and, 61–62
  Lean Mastery (Stage 3) and, 64
  Lean Transformation (Stage 4) and, 65–66
  learning mindset, 72
  nurturing, 71–72
  as role models, 44–45
  values, 72
The Leadership Challenge (Kouzes and Posner), 45
"Leading Change in Challenging Times", 39
Leading Change (Kotter), 37
"The Lean Approach to Management" (Balle and Chartier), 37
Lean as a holistic philosophy, 30
Lean assimilation, 62–64; *see also* continuous improvement maturity model
lean initiation, 61–62
"Lean in name only", 30
Lean manufacturing, 17
Lean Mastery, 64–65
Lean Revolution, 51–53
Lean Six Sigma, 53–54
Lean thinking, 30, 54–55, 61
Lean Thinking (Womack and Jones), 36
Lean transformation, 1–19
  CIMM, 65–67
  decluttering, 2
  employee participation, 7–8
  failure (case study of NUMMI), 9–12
  focus areas, 4–5

implementing, 2, 6–7
management and, 8–9
plan (eight steps), 5–6
as popular approach, 17
success (case study of Toyota), 3, 12–15
as systematic approach, 2
why companies fail, 15–16
learning ecosystem, 44
learning opportunities, 78
learning organization, 39–40, 46
Lee, Jonathan, 40
long-term measurement, 40

M

manufacturing industry, 121
Martinez, Susan, 40
matrix organizational structures, 113
McDonald's Corporation
glocalization, 124
streamlining processes, 124–125
McKinsey & Company research/study, 24–26, 39
McKinsey Quarterly, 2
measurement systems, 32, 48
CIMM framework, 78
long-term, 40
Microsoft, 94–95
mindset, 4
mindset and priorities, 42–43
Mitchell, Sarah, 37
Morita, Akio, 3
motivation, 13

N

Netflix, 48
net promoter score (NPS), 121
New United Motor Manufacturing Inc. (NUMMI), 9–12
Nobeoka, Kentaro, 36
NPS, *see* Net promoter score
NUMMI, *see* New United Motor Manufacturing Inc.

O

Ohno, Taiichi, 1, 8, 12–13, 60
one-size-fits-all approach, 129–130
optimizing processes, 128–129
organizational structures
assessment, 113
centralized *vs.* decentralized, 113
flexibility, 113
hierarchical structures, 113
matrix, 113
scaling and adaptability of CIMM, 112–114
overlooking small wins, 31–32

P

perceptions and data, 55–57
performance management
integrating improvement into, 43
traditional evaluation, 43
PharmaMed, 97–98
Pixar
collaborative culture of, 47
Plan Do Check Act (PDCA), 6
Poka-Yoke, 13–14
Porsche, 8
Portfolio Kanban, 5–6
Posner, Barry Z., 45
problem-solving framework, 38
"The Problem with Lean: A Reflection on How Lean Became the Victim of Its Own Success", 35
The Progress Principle (Amabile), 41
"The Psychology of Change Management", 2

Q

quantifiable success stories, 97–101
GlobalLogistics, 99–100
PharmaMed, 97–98
SuperMart, 100–101
VitaMed, 98–99

R

real-world stories of CIMM's application/adoption, 83–101
global organizations, 84–88
local business ventures, 88–101
overview, 83–85
regard for individuals, 13
regulations, *see* laws and regulations

research and development (R&D) network, 125–126; *see also* BASF SE
resilience, 111
  adaptive leadership, 135, 138
resistance to change, 3
resource allocation, 107
RetailCo, 93–94
retail sector, 121
Rodriguez, Maria, 38
root cause analysis, 38
Roser, Christoph, 10

S

Sahota, Michael, 41
scalability, 103–112, 137–138
  challenges and considerations, 106–108
  cultural diversity, 107–108, 114–115
  defined, 105
  enabling sustainable growth, 105
  essence of, 105–106
  flexibility, 107–109
  harmonizing global operations, 106
  implications, 109–110
  laws and regulations, 106–107
  organizational structures, 112–114
  standardization, 106–109
  sustainable growth, 111–112
Schein, Edgar, 62
Schwab, Charles, 54
situational approach, 4
Smith, John, 34
standardization
  benefits, 108
  scaling CIMM, 106–109
statistical evidence
  Amazon, 92–93
  E-Trade Emporium, 92–93
  Toyota, 92–93
Stellar Call Center, 89–90
stories of CIMM's application/adoption, *see* real-world stories of CIMM's application/adoption
SuperMart, 100–101
sustainable growth, 111–112; *see also* scalability

T

technology, 47–48; *see also* innovation
  scaling CIMM, 107
  sector, 121
TechWave, 96–97
Thompson, James, 38
Thompson, Jennifer, 41
Toffler, Alvin, 65
Toyoda, Kiichiro, 13
Toyota, 33, 68
  CIMM, 67, 86–88, 92–93
  Lean transformation, 3, 12–15, 45–46
  NUMMI, 9–12
Toyota Production System (TPS), 3, 11–13, 33, 60, 62, 86, 127
traditional lean methodologies, 127–128
  CIMM *vs.*, 129–131
  limitations of, 128–129
  principles and concepts, 127–128
training and education, 31, 44, 61–62
transformative narratives, *see* real-world stories of CIMM's application/adoption
Trumpf, 8
Turner, Sophia, 60

U

"U-Curve" model (Unilever), 123
Unilever, 123

V

value, holistic view of, 37–38
value stream mapping, 5, 63
VitaMed, 98–99

W

Welch, Jack, 46
Wenger-Trayner, Etienne, 44
Wheatley, Margaret, 64
"Why Celebrate? Benefits of Celebration in Organizations", 44
Williams, Sandra, 39
Womack, James, 36